Current
CONTROVERSIES

The U.S. Economy

DATE DUE

Other Books in the Current Controversies Series

The U.S. Economy

Debra A. Miller, Book Editor

GREENHAVEN PRESS

A part of Gale, Cengage Learning

Detroit • New York • San Francisco • New Haven, Conn • Waterville, Maine • London

GALE
CENGAGE Learning

Christine Nasso, *Publisher*
Elizabeth Des Chenes, *Managing Editor*

© 2010 Greenhaven Press, a part of Gale, Cengage Learning

Gale and Greenhaven Press are registered trademarks used herein under license.

For more information, contact:
Greenhaven Press
27500 Drake Rd.
Farmington Hills, MI 48331-3535
Or you can visit our Internet site at gale.cengage.com

ALL RIGHTS RESERVED.
No part of this work covered by the copyright herein may be reproduced, transmitted, stored, or used in any form or by any means graphic, electronic, or mechanical, including but not limited to photocopying, recording, scanning, digitizing, taping, Web distribution, information networks, or information storage and retrieval systems, except as permitted under Section 107 or 108 of the 1976 United States Copyright Act, without the prior written permission of the publisher.

For product information and technology assistance, contact us at

Gale Customer Support, 1-800-877-4253
For permission to use material from this text or product, submit all requests online at www.cengage.com/permissions

Further permissions questions can be emailed to permissionrequest@cengage.com

Articles in Greenhaven Press anthologies are often edited for length to meet page requirements. In addition, original titles of these works are changed to clearly present the main thesis and to explicitly indicate the author's opinion. Every effort is made to ensure that Greenhaven Press accurately reflects the original intent of the authors. Every effort has been made to trace the owners of copyrighted material.

Cover image copyright © Najlah Feanny/Corbis.

LIBRARY OF CONGRESS CATALOGING-IN-PUBLICATION DATA

The U.S. economy / Debra A. Miller, book editor.
   p. cm. -- (Current controversies)
   Includes bibliographical references and index.
   ISBN 978-0-7377-4711-9 (hbk.) -- ISBN 978-0-7377-4712-6 (pbk.)
   1. United States--Economic policy--2009---Juvenile literature. 2. United States--Economic conditions--2009--Juvenile literature. 3. Global Financial Crisis, 2008-2009--Juvenile literature. 4. Recessions--United States--Juvenile literature. I. Miller, Debra A.
   HC106.84.U155 2010
   330.973--dc22
                                         2009050764

ACC LIBRARY SERVICES
AUSTIN, TX

Printed in the United States of America
1 2 3 4 5 6 7 14 13 12 11 10

Contents

Chapter 1: Are There Serious Problems with the U.S. Economy?

Yes: There Are Serious Problems with the U.S. Economy

John Paul Rossi

> The American economy in 2008 began spiraling down a path very similar to the one that resulted in the Great Depression of the 1930s. The collapse of a speculatory real estate bubble has caused mortgage and financial crises that have constricted credit, cut off business investment, and curtailed consumer spending.

Julie Haviv

> The U.S. housing market is in a severe slump marked by dropping home values, tight lending standards, and record foreclosures. The housing crisis is the primary source of the U.S. economic recession and its end is not yet in sight.

Douglas J. Elliott

> The bank "stress tests" conducted by the U.S. government concluded that the nation's largest banks are strong enough to survive without large amounts of new capital. Banks remain vulnerable, however, so the bank solvency crisis and the credit crunch are not about to end anytime soon.

Chapter 3: Is the Growing U.S. Debt a Threat to Americans?

Foreword

By definition, controversies are "discussions of questions in which opposing opinions clash" (Webster's Twentieth Century Dictionary Unabridged). Few would deny that controversies are a pervasive part of the human condition and exist on virtually every level of human enterprise. Controversies transpire between individuals and among groups, within nations and between nations. Controversies supply the grist necessary for progress by providing challenges and challengers to the status quo. They also create atmospheres where strife and warfare can flourish. A world without controversies would be a peaceful world; but it also would be, by and large, static and prosaic.

The Series' Purpose

The purpose of the Current Controversies series is to explore many of the social, political, and economic controversies dominating the national and international scenes today. Titles selected for inclusion in the series are highly focused and specific. For example, from the larger category of criminal justice, Current Controversies deals with specific topics such as police brutality, gun control, white collar crime, and others. The debates in Current Controversies also are presented in a useful, timeless fashion. Articles and book excerpts included in each title are selected if they contribute valuable, long-range ideas to the overall debate. And wherever possible, current information is enhanced with historical documents and other relevant materials. Thus, while individual titles are current in focus, every effort is made to ensure that they will not become quickly outdated. Books in the Current Controversies series will remain important resources for librarians, teachers, and students for many years.

In addition to keeping the titles focused and specific, great care is taken in the editorial format of each book in the series. Book introductions and chapter prefaces are offered to provide background material for readers. Chapters are organized around several key questions that are answered with diverse opinions representing all points on the political spectrum. Materials in each chapter include opinions in which authors clearly disagree as well as alternative opinions in which authors may agree on a broader issue but disagree on the possible solutions. In this way, the content of each volume in Current Controversies mirrors the mosaic of opinions encountered in society. Readers will quickly realize that there are many viable answers to these complex issues. By questioning each author's conclusions, students and casual readers can begin to develop the critical thinking skills so important to evaluating opinionated material.

Current Controversies is also ideal for controlled research. Each anthology in the series is composed of primary sources taken from a wide gamut of informational categories including periodicals, newspapers, books, U.S. and foreign government documents, and the publications of private and public organizations. Readers will find factual support for reports, debates, and research papers covering all areas of important issues. In addition, an annotated table of contents, an index, a book and periodical bibliography, and a list of organizations to contact are included in each book to expedite further research.

Perhaps more than ever before in history, people are confronted with diverse and contradictory information. During the Persian Gulf War, for example, the public was not only treated to minute-to-minute coverage of the war, it was also inundated with critiques of the coverage and countless analyses of the factors motivating U.S. involvement. Being able to sort through the plethora of opinions accompanying today's major issues, and to draw one's own conclusions, can be a complicated and frustrating struggle. It is the editors' hope that Current Controversies will help readers with this struggle.

Introduction

> *"Most observers agree that the primary cause of the U.S. recession was a collapse of the U.S. housing market, which in turn was sparked by defaults in the subprime lending market."*

According to the National Bureau of Economic Research (NBER), a nonpartisan economic research organization based in Massachusetts, a recession is defined as a significant, protracted decline in economic activity that spreads throughout the country, affecting various economic indicators such as income, employment, retail sales, and industrial production. Beginning in late 2006 and early 2007, U.S. policy makers started to see some of these signs of recession in the U.S economy. Housing prices, which had been rising for many years, fell rapidly, for example, and the number of unemployed workers began inching upward. Conditions quickly deteriorated further as months passed. The stock market plummeted and by the fall of 2008, many large banks and other important financial institutions in the United States—including giant government-chartered mortgage lending companies Fannie Mae and Freddie Mac, financial services firm Lehman Brothers Holdings Inc., and insurer American International Group, Inc. (AIG)—came close to bankruptcy. On December 1, 2008, NBER officially declared that the country had been in a recession since December 2007.

Responding to the growing crisis, the U.S. Federal Reserve, the nation's central bank in charge of regulating the money supply, cut its short-term interest rate several times in 2007. In that same year, the George W. Bush administration negotiated an economic stimulus plan with Congress that sent out income tax rebate checks of as much as $1200 for couples, plus $300 per child. In October 2008, the federal government authorized $700 billion in federal funding for the Troubled Asset Relief Program (TARP)—a massive program to rescue failing banks. Another federal program, known as the Term Asset-Backed Securities Loan Facility (TALF), allowed the Federal Reserve to help ease credit and pressures on financial markets by purchasing mortgage-backed securities, commercial bonds of companies, and assets held by nonbank financial institutions, such as credit card or auto loan companies.

In January 2009, facing the worst economic crisis since the Great Depression of the 1930s, the incoming Barack Obama administration worked with Congress to pass another economic stimulus bill, the American Recovery and Reinvestment Act—a $787 billion package designed to boost economic growth with a mixture of tax cuts, aid to states, and infrastructure spending. Under President Obama, the government also continued to spend TARP and TALF monies to bail out banks and other financial institutions. In addition, federal funds were spent to save the U.S. auto industry, guarantee loans for small businesses, and provide assistance for homeowners to refinance mortgages. At the same time, the Federal Reserve directly bought up U.S. debt to lower interest rates. By the summer of 2009, many economists voiced optimism that these government strategies might be having some effect and that the economy had begun to recover, as unemployment rates and home foreclosures slowed and banks and other financial institutions began to report better profit figures.

Most observers agree that the primary cause of the U.S. recession was a collapse of the U.S. housing market, which in turn was sparked by defaults in the subprime lending market—a sector of home loans made to buyers with very little or no verification of their income or assets. Many of these buyers bought homes they really could not afford by taking out adjustable rate loans that had a very low beginning interest rate that could adjust upward later in the loan period. Other loans were interest-only during the first few years and some were 100 percent financed with no down payment. This risky strategy worked for many homeowners, because most homes escalated in value during what was a booming housing market in the years after 2001, allowing homeowners to refinance their loans before higher interest rates or higher monthly payments kicked in. Other homeowners were not so lucky and got stuck with high mortgage payments when housing prices began to fall.

Home buyers taking on too much risk, however, was not the only cause of the recession. Most analysts agree that mortgage companies, banks, Wall Street investors, and even the U.S. government also played significant roles. For example, many commentators have noted that the housing boom started largely because the Federal Reserve kept interest rates extremely low for many years—a policy that created the easy credit that allowed almost anyone to buy a home. For their part, many mortgage originators and lending banks encouraged individuals to apply for the high-risk subprime loans, because the loans could be bundled together and sold to investors for large fees. The circle of risk was made complete when important Wall Street investment banks and other large investment companies began buying the mortgage bundles, repackaging and advertising them as high quality, low-risk, mortgage-backed securities that they in turn sold for large profits around the world. Even Fannie Mac and Freddie Mac, entities created by the government, joined in the purchase and creation of bundled mortgage securities. Significantly, the government imposed no limitations on these new securities, and there was no meaningful oversight by the Securities and Exchange Commission—the federal agency charged with regulating securities—or Congress. Some commentators have attributed the lack of regulation to policy makers' desire to free up loan money to enable more Americans to buy their own homes.

As long as housing prices continued to rise and buyers did not default on their mortgage loans, the housing bubble stayed afloat and each player in the system made money. Homeowners were thrilled to watch their property values soar year after year, and some Wall Street traders routinely made bonuses of $160 million or more each year. The rising home prices also appeared to be good for the overall economy, because homeowners could borrow against their increasing home equity to make other consumer purchases, such as cars, vacations, or home improvements. However, when home prices dropped and foreclosures began, the housing bubble burst, and the entire U.S. economy began to unravel. Homeowners could no longer refinance their subprime mortgages and many found themselves committed to mortgages they could not pay or worse, "upside-down"—a term used when the amount owed on the mortgage is more than the value of the home. Mortgage companies no longer had any business; large banks and other investment entities suddenly found themselves with millions of bad loans on their books; and investors in the U.S. stock market watched as their portfolios dropped by half. The failing U.S. economy also quickly affected other countries that had invested in the U.S. housing securities or that depended on exports to the United States.

The U.S. economic crisis and what to do about it have now become hotly debated topics among experts, policy makers, and the public. The authors of *Current Controversies: The U.S. Economy* address some of the questions raised by the recession, including whether the U.S. economy is in serious trouble, whether President Barack Obama's economic policies are working, whether the increasing U.S. deficit is a problem, and what economic policies should be followed in the future.

CHAPTER 1

Are There Serious Problems with the U.S. Economy?

Chapter Preface

When the U.S. economy sank into what appeared to be a deep recession in 2007, 2008, and 2009, many commentators described it as the worst economic crisis since the 1930s. Some people even wondered whether the United States was entering into another major depression like the Great Depression, a devastating worldwide economic collapse that occurred following the U.S. stock market crash in 1929. Despite certain similarities between the two economic crises, however, most economists believe that it is unlikely that today's recession will worsen into a depression. They reason that this economic crisis is not nearly as widespread across the economy as the Great Depression, but also that policy makers have learned important lessons about how to handle economic slowdowns.

Still, the current recession is decidedly much worse than any economic downturn within the last fiftyyears. The United States has experienced two other serious recessions in recent years—one from 1973 to 1975 and another during the years of 1981 and 1982. Each of those crises lasted a mere sixteen months, while today's recession has already exceeded that time period, since it began in December 2007. In addition, the 2007–2009 recession is deeper than the previous two downturns, causing 86 percent of U.S. industries to cut back on production, increasing unemployment in every state and causing a drop in household wealth larger than any since the end of World War II.

Despite the severity of the recession, however, according to most economic experts, the United States is not even close to the drop in economic activity recorded during the Great Depression. According to the *New York Times*, the U.S. gross domestic product (GDP)—a popular measure of a country's economic output—has only dropped about 1.7 percent in this recession, compared to the 26.5 percent drop in GDP that occurred during the Great Depression years of 1929 to 1933. Even if economic activity continues to decline, experts have predicted that it will not likely drop more than about 3.4 percent over the life of the recession. This level of slowdown is definitely worse than any experienced over the last several decades, but it still comes nowhere near to matching the Great Depression figure. Also, although the United States has seen a huge drop in the housing market, a decline in household wealth, and severe weakness in the financial sector, many analysts say the overall U.S. economy is still strong and likely to weather the current crisis.

Most importantly, after the Great Depression, the federal government began to play a much more active role in ensuring economic stability, putting in place a number of safeguards that help to prevent rapid declines into major depressions. Some of these safeguards are government-funded safety net programs such as unemployment insurance, food stamps, and Social Security, which help people who lose their jobs or are squeezed financially during recessionary times. Increased government regulation of the economy, especially of financial markets, is another check on the economy that helps to ensure greater economic stability. For example, the United States established the Securities and Exchange Commission (SEC) in 1934 to regulate stock market trading. Another regulatory safeguard was the Banking Act of 1933 (also known as the Glass-Steagall Act), which insured bank deposits and prohibited banks from underwriting or dealing in securities. Since then, banking panics like those seen during the Great Depression, when large numbers of people withdrew their money from banks based on fears that the banks would go bankrupt, have been largely eliminated as an exacerbating factor in recessions.

The federal government also embraced new policy ideas to temper economic downturns following the depression of the 1930s. One of these was to follow economic theories developed by British economist John Maynard Keynes, who in the 1930s suggested that increases in government spending, tax cuts, and monetary expansion (that is, increasing the money supply) could be used to counteract depressions. Since then, U.S. government officials have routinely used these tools to attempt to manage the economy and prevent major disruptions. During the 2007–2009 U.S. recession, for example, the government has wasted no time in implementing several Keynesian programs to inject vitality into the sinking economy. One example is the $787 billion stimulus bill passed by Congress in February 2009. In addition, the U.S. Federal Reserve, led by Great Depression expert Ben Bernanke, has pumped trillions of dollars into the economy with new lending programs designed to increase the money supply. The government has also avoided some of the mistakes made during the Great Depression that worsened the economic decline, such as government price controls and trade tariffs.

Nevertheless, the recession continues to be painful for many Americans, and economists cannot come to a consensus about when it will end. Even if a positive economic recovery occurs in coming months and years, some economists are predicting that the recovery might be weak and that the country could enter a period of prolonged economic stagnation similar to what occurred in Japan during the 1990s. In the case of Japan's so-called "lost decade," the economy failed to recover from a recession despite the fact that the government funded substantial infrastructure and other spending projects. The authors of the viewpoints in this chapter present differing views about the state of the U.S. economy and when it is likely to recover.

The U.S. Economy Is in the Worst Financial Crisis Since the Great Depression

John Paul Rossi

John Paul Rossi is an associate professor of history at Penn State Erie, the Behrend College. He is also a writer for the History News Service, a syndicate of professional historians who seek to improve the public's understanding of current events by setting these events in their historical contexts.

The United States is in the midst of the worst financial crisis since the Great Depression. The question is: How close are we to another Great Depression?

The answer is: Very close. Here's why.

Similar to the Great Depression

The Great Depression was the result of the combination of the 1929 financial crisis and serious structural problems in the American economy such as widespread poverty. After the 1929 stock market collapse, these factors cut deeply into business investment and personal consumption. The consequence was a downward spiral that created the worst economic collapse in American history.

Today's economy is hurtling downward on a similar path. The mortgage and financial crises have constricted credit and largely cut off business investment. Stagnant wages and over-borrowing have curtailed consumer spending.

The collapse of a stock market bubble in 1929 triggered the chain of events that led to depression. When stock prices fell in October 1929, investors, financial institutions and banks were caught overextended. The fall in stock prices produced a

John Paul Rossi, "Another Great Depression?" History News Service, November 27, 2008. www.h-net.org. Reproduced by permission.

financial panic that bankrupted many. To repair damaged balance sheets, surviving banks and financiers dramatically reduced lending. The result was a long and steep decline in economic activity.

Much as in 1929, the 2008 collapse has been the consequence of a speculatory bubble, this time in real estate. It was pumped up by overlending by banks and financial companies and overborrowing by Wall Street. Rising interest rates helped burst the bubble. Subsequent property owner defaults caught investors, financiers and businesses holding mortgages, or investments based on them, short. Enormous losses for investment firms and banks followed. Despite government bailouts and aid, the country's surviving major banks have severely cut lending.

The 1920s' stock market bubble hid serious structural problems in the underlying economy. The same is true for the real estate bubble in the 2000s.

Similar Decline in Income and Consumer Demand

In the 1920s widespread poverty and an inequitable distribution of wealth contributed to the depression of the next decade. In 1929, 42 percent of American families were living in severe poverty. Consumer credit provided some purchasing power to those in society's bottom half, but by the end of the 1920s that group had exhausted its borrowing power. The bulk of the U.S. economy's income went to the top 1 percent of the nation's families, who earned the same amount as the combined income of the bottom 40 percent.

A similar situation occurred at the end of the 1990s when workers' wages stagnated while the income of the wealthiest Americans rose. By 2003 the distribution of income had reached the 1929 point, with the richest 1 percent of families receiving the same income as the bottom 40 percent.

The decline of working Americans' income was somewhat masked by rising real estate and stock prices, as well as the rapid extension of consumer credit. To maintain their standard of living, middle-class Americans turned to borrowing more through credit cards and home equity loans. By 2006 these practices had turned Americans' savings rate negative— its worst performance since the Great Depression—as many spent more than they earned.

The 1929 financial collapse combined with poverty and the distribution of income to significantly cut spending for all levels of American society. Demand was down, businesses could not get the credit needed to finance operations and employees were laid off. Declines in business and worker income followed, consumption dropped, and firms went bankrupt. This caused yet more banks to fail and created a downward spiral.

The economy is rapidly spiraling downward into the next great depression.

A similar process is underway now. The collapse of housing and stock prices and the credit freeze cut off borrowing as a means to support middle-class consumption. Even worse, too many of those who overborrowed are unable to pay; they're now defaulting on their mortgages, car loans, and credit-card debts. The result is rapidly falling levels of spending and consumption. These consumption declines are merging with the constriction of bank credit; many companies cannot get even short-term loans to carry on operations.

Much as was the case in 1929 the twin declines of consumer and business spending are rippling through the economy. They're causing worker income and general consumption to fall and bringing on mounting layoffs. As unemployment rises, more individuals will be unable to pay their debts and additional personal and business bankruptcies will follow. This means more bank and investment company failures and bailouts.

The American economy in 2008 is following the same path it took in 1929. The collapse of a speculatory bubble has merged with problems of the distribution of wealth, working Americans' incomes and consumption. The consequence is that the economy is rapidly spiraling downward into the next great depression.

The U.S. Housing Market Is in a Terrible Slump

Julie Haviv

Julie Haviv is a reporter for Reuters, an international news service.

The U.S. housing market slump is nowhere near over and home prices will probably keep falling well into next year [2010], one of the property market's best-known economists said.

Karl Case, the codeveloper of a widely watched gauge of the housing industry, told Reuters that the hard-hit U.S. housing market has gone from being the primary source of the U.S. economic recession to one of its biggest casualties.

"Never say never, but it is looking increasingly probable that we will not see a housing market bottom until next year," said Case, an economics professor at Wellesley College in Massachusetts.

"If the housing market was independent of the economy, we would be getting closer to a bottom, but that is not the case and we have a horrible economy," he said in an interview late on Tuesday [February 24, 2009].

A Record Decline

The United States has been in recession for more than a year. The fourth quarter [of 2008] showed the biggest economic contraction since 1982.

The Standard & Poor's S&P/Case-Shiller Home Price Indices, [a monitoring tool] which Case codeveloped, has shown an acceleration in the fall-off in home prices in recent months.

Case, whose research has focused on real estate markets and prices for over 20 years, said he did not anticipate the ex-

Julie Haviv, "U.S. Housing Market Bottom May Be a Year Away: Case," Reuters UK, February 26, 2009. Reproduced by permission.

tent of home price depreciation that has transpired since the peak in the second quarter of 2006.

The U.S. housing market is in the worst downturn since the Great Depression.

"I did not think it was probable that we would have a home price decline of this magnitude," he said.

Standard & Poor's said on Tuesday the S&P/Case-Shiller 20-City Composite Index was down a record 18.5 percent in December, with home prices on a month-over-month basis falling 2.5 percent in December from November, compared with a 2.3 percent decline in the previous period. The 20-city index dates to 2000.

S&P said its 10-City Composite Index declined 2.3 percent in December from November, compared with a 2.2 percent decline in the previous period, for a 19.2 percent drop year over year—also a record for the index, which dates back to 1988. From the peak in the second quarter of 2006, average home prices are down 26.7 percent, S&P said.

The U.S. housing market is in the worst downturn since the Great Depression as a huge supply of unsold homes, tighter lending standards, and record mortgage foreclosures push down home prices. Its impact has rippled through the recession-hit economy, as well as to the rest of the world.

The strongest government action yet to aid homeowners since the housing market's meltdown began is targeting just the right areas, Case said.

President Barack Obama last week [February 2009] announced a plan to back refinancing for reliable borrowers; help distressed borrowers avoid foreclosure; and stimulate new housing demand through the expansion of housing finance giants Fannie Mae and Freddie Mac. Case said if he were to grade the housing plan he would give it an "A."

"While it does not have a high likelihood of making a big difference, it does have a high likelihood of making some difference and that is exactly the right thing to do," he said.

Foreclosure sales have dragged overall home prices down. But fewer foreclosures help assuage one of the housing market's biggest banes, which is a huge supply of unsold homes.

"In six months we will probably begin to see something happen in the pipeline of foreclosures and any impact that may have on home prices," Case said.

The Solvency Crisis for U.S. Banks May Be Far from Over

Douglas J. Elliott

Douglas J. Elliott is a fellow in economic studies with the Initiative on Business and Public Policy, a project of the Brookings Institution, a public policy think tank.

The financial "stress tests" on the big banks [conducted by the U.S. government in 2009] gave us good news: They "only" need $75 billion of new capital. That's a lot of money, but much less than many of us feared. However, it is important not to take excessive comfort from what is essentially a highly educated guess as to the future of the banks in a very uncertain environment. We've never been in a crisis like this and we simply don't know how it will play out. If the stress test's estimates of the value of the banks' assets at the end of 2010 were off by just 3%, we'd need another $300 billion of capital.

Painful Possibilities

What you think about the stress test results depends heavily on how tough you think the test was. My own view is that, everything taken together, there is roughly a two in three chance that the banks will do as well or better than the stress test results. The problem is that the other one in three chance includes some very painful possibilities, such as those projected by Dr. Nouriel Roubini of NYU [New York University], who is probably the most pessimistic of the analysts who have made really detailed loss estimates.

The stress test was somewhat tougher than the projections of the International Monetary Fund (IMF) [an international

Douglas J. Elliott, "Bank Stress Test Results," *Huffington Post*, May 12, 2009. Reproduced by permission.

lending organization], which has done a very thorough analysis that epitomizes the "consensus" view by economists of the banking system's near-term future. The IMF analysis implies about $300 billion of credit losses still to come at the big banks, which would be covered by about $200 billion of new earnings, excluding those credit losses, plus about $100 billion of new capital that has been or will soon be raised. In other words, the IMF figures imply that the banks have about bottomed out.

Many people have the perception that the IMF figures were much larger, so let me briefly explain the $300 billion in credit losses. The IMF believes there will be massive credit losses worldwide of $4.1 trillion. However, all but $1.1 trillion of that will fall on foreigners and nonbanks. Half of the remainder is losses that have already been taken. When you scale down the remaining $550 billion to represent the share of the 19 banks in the stress test, it comes down to $321 billion, by my estimate.

Even if the big banks are . . . strong enough to survive reasonably soundly without raising large amounts of capital, it does not mean the credit crunch is about to end anytime soon.

So, the stress tests were tougher than "consensus" estimates. However, it was not nearly as tough as the projections of the real pessimists. Roubini's loss estimates imply not the break-even results from the IMF, but a need for almost $500 billion of additional capital. If he is even close to being correct, we are far from finished with the solvency crisis at the banks.

Even if the big banks are indeed now strong enough to survive reasonably soundly without raising large amounts of capital, it does not mean the credit crunch is about to end anytime soon. The test was to see if banks could hit their target minimum capital ratios by the end of 2010 at their current size, which implies roughly their current level of lending. If we find ourselves in the stress scenario or worse, which is maybe a one in three chance, banks will not have room to expand their lending and may need to contract.

All in all, the [bank] stress tests were useful and the results were encouraging. However, we have a lot of pain to get through before this crisis is over.

What makes this much worse is that the "shadow banking" market used to provide about 40% of all loans, but has contracted very sharply. We need the banks to be strong enough to fill the gap by making more loans and keeping them on their books. This would require far more capital, which will only become available when the financial markets become much more willing to fund the banks at reasonable prices. Bank stocks are doing much better in the last couple of weeks, but the market is far from strong enough to handle hundreds of billions of dollars of new capital requirements at the banks.

Dealing with Toxic Assets

The stress tests also mean that it will be even harder to successfully implement the government's new programs to deal with toxic assets. The banks are generally unfavorable to this program and the test results will ease the pressure on them to participate. They believe that private investors, even with generous incentives from the taxpayers, will not be willing to pay what these distressed assets are actually worth. The banks genuinely believe that while the assets have lost a lot of value, they remain worth perhaps 60% of their face value on average. Investors were willing to pay about 30 cents on the dollar before the programs and the incentives might kick this up to 40 or 45 cents.

It is going to be hard to push most of the banks to participate, since the stress test just said they will have enough capital to get through even a tough economic environment, while holding onto the toxic assets. Regulators in America have the right to push banks to do things that are necessary to keep them solvent, but not to overturn business decisions otherwise. In practice, a few of the big banks are highly vulnerable to regulatory pressure and may participate for that reason. The others may choose not to play or will do so only half-heartedly.

All in all, the stress tests were useful and the results were encouraging. However, we have a lot of pain to get through before this crisis is over. If we're lucky, it will remain bad for awhile. If we're unlucky, and Roubini is right, it could still get extremely ugly.

The Deteriorating U.S. Economy Is Swelling the Ranks of the Homeless

Oliver Burkeman

Oliver Burkeman writes news and features for the Guardian, *a British newspaper.*

For years, Joan Burke has had to battle the fact that homelessness, for most Americans, is an invisible scourge. Recently, however, invisibility hasn't exactly been the problem.

Ten minutes' walk from where she works, at the homelessness charity Loaves & Fishes, in Sacramento, California, lies an all-too-visible "tent city"—a shantytown, built on wasteground beside railway tracks, that has become one of the most prominent symbols of the recession.

The Recession's Tent Cities

Tent cities reminiscent of the "Hoovervilles" of the Great Depression have been springing up in cities across the United States—from Reno in Nevada to Tampa in Florida—as foreclosures and redundancies force middle-class families from their homes.

"Where the tent city is now is literally a toxic waste dump, it's unsafe, but these people are very resourceful," Burke said. "Some people are living in squalor, with just a tarp tied to a chain-link fence. But then you'll see someone with several tents: The tent they live in, plus some outbuilding tents. And they couldn't be more neat and more tidy. They're working hard to create a sense of home."

Oliver Burkeman, "US Tent Cities Highlight New Realities as Recession Wears On," *Guardian*, March 26, 2009. www.guardian.co.uk. Reproduced by permission of Guardian News Service, LTD.

Many of the 200 residents of Sacramento's Tent City, as with those around the country, are not recent victims of the downturn: They are the chronically homeless, some of them mentally ill. But the encampment seized national attention after Oprah Winfrey featured it on her daytime television show, part of a series of reports she has been running on the "new faces" of homelessness.

Embarrassed by an influx of television crews, Arnold Schwarzenegger [California's governor] this week [March 26, 2009] announced plans to house the tent-dwellers in a nearby convention centre until a $1m [million] plan for more permanent shelter can be implemented.

The California governor told reporters he had "personally delivered a letter to President Barack Obama last week, to request that economic stimulus funds for the homeless be fast-tracked".

In both the number and types of inhabitants, the new tent cities do not equate to the homelessness of the 1930s. But the symbolism is powerful.

Obama grappled with the phenomenon on Tuesday, when a reporter at his prime-time news conference asked him about the "tent cities sprouting up across the country". The president said he was "heartbroken that any child in America is homeless", adding: "The most important thing I can do on their behalf is to make sure their parents have a job."

Similarities to the Great Depression

In both the number and types of inhabitants, the new tent cities do not equate to the homelessness of the 1930s. But the symbolism is powerful, and may have significant political consequences. It was not all that far from Sacramento, or from Fresno—home to another Californian tent city—that the celebrated Depression-era photographer Dorothea Lange took her haunting photos of families living in makeshift camps, forced west by the collapsed economy and the Dust Bowl further east.

"We all take care of each other," Michelle Holbrook, a 34-year-old resident of the Sacramento camp who lost her job as a carer [caregiver], told the *San Jose Mercury News*. "I've become the camp mother: I do most of the cooking, and make hot water for coffee." A resident of Reno's tent city, Tammy, said: "We eat things that other people throw out, or whatever . . . It's really embarrassing to say, but that's the way it sometimes is out here." Another Reno tent-dweller, Jim, told one of Oprah's reporters it was "like learning how to live all over again".

Obama's stimulus package includes $1.5bn [billion] for emergency shelters, and, if passed, his budget should significantly expand funding for affordable housing. Philip Mangano, director of the US Interagency Council on Homelessness, has called the stimulus funds "manna from heaven", saying they would boost his two-pronged strategy of preventing homelessness while rapidly rehousing those who fall victim to it. Last year, the US government reported that homelessness in America had declined by 30% between 2005 and 2007.

The changing economy has . . . thrown very different kinds of people into close quarters with one another.

Burke, whose organisation provides food and shower facilities for Sacramento's Tent City residents, has mixed feelings about the national media exposure. It may help build support for addressing the problem, she said, but also threatens to reinforce a distinction between the "deserving" victims of the recession and those who have been homeless for longer, and for other reasons.

"It's an oddity of human nature that we are more about people who have suffered for a short time, rather than people who have suffered for a long time," she said. "When we can identify with somebody's situation, obviously, our empathy is engaged quickly: You can look at someone and say, 'You know, goodness, they owned their own home, they look like I do.' But if someone's been homeless for a while, they no longer look like we think we look. If you're living in a tent, it doesn't take long before you're somewhat unkempt and dirty, because you're living in the dirt."

The changing economy has, accordingly, thrown very different kinds of people into close quarters with one another. In Fresno, freelance electricians and truck drivers, employed until months ago, rub shoulders with crack addicts and those with serious psychological problems. There have been reports of violence in one part of Fresno's encampment, known as New Jack City, but Burke said what really impressed her in Sacramento was the degree of cooperation.

"There is a sort of very pure democracy and self-governance at play. People are making up the rules of their cluster of tents, deciding what's permitted, just as in any sort of community," she said. "You don't want to romanticise this—it isn't camping—but there is a community, and there is a sense of helping others. We've had a series of storms here recently, and if there's somebody new who doesn't have a tent, people will take them in. It's that understanding that, you know, there's somebody worse off than I am."

The Recession Is Global and Deeper than Previously Thought

Timothy R. Homan and Simon Kennedy

Timothy R. Homan and Simon Kennedy are reporters for Bloomberg.com, a financial Web site.

April 22 (Bloomberg)—The International Monetary Fund said the global recession will be deeper and the recovery slower than previously thought as financial markets take longer to stabilize.

The Washington-based IMF said in a forecast released today that the world economy will shrink 1.3 percent this year, compared with its January projection of 0.5 percent growth. The lender predicted expansion of 1.9 percent next year instead of its earlier 3 percent estimate.

The fund's latest outlook highlights the precarious state in which the world economy remains, even amid signs the worst slump since World War II may be easing. Recovery isn't assured and will depend on policy efforts to cleanse banks' balance sheets and craft measures that spur demand, the IMF said.

"The key factor determining the course of the downturn and recovery will be the rate of progress toward returning the financial sector to health," the fund said in its semi-annual World Economic Outlook. At a briefing in Washington, IMF Chief Economist Olivier Blanchard said while a recovery will start early next year, a "return to normal" will take much longer.

Having said this time last year that the world economy would grow 3.8 percent in 2009, the IMF tied its more pessimistic assessment to a "recognition that financial stabilization will take longer than previously envisaged." Managing Director Dominique Strauss-Kahn foreshadowed the prediction of a contraction a month ago.

Credit Losses

The revised outlook comes a day after the fund calculated worldwide losses from distressed loans and securitized assets may reach $4.1 trillion by the end of 2010 as the recession and credit crunch exact a higher toll on financial institutions.

"Financial strains in the mature markets will remain heavy well into 2010," that report said.

U.S. regulators are putting some of the largest U.S. banks through so-called stress tests to determine the amount of capital each needs to withstand a further economic slide. Morgan Stanley today reported a bigger-than-estimated $177 million loss and slashed its dividend to 5 cents as real estate and debt-related write-downs overwhelmed trading gains.

Even as the IMF acknowledged "tentative indications" that the rate of contraction is moderating around the world, the fund said output per capita would decline this year in countries representing about 75 percent of the global economy.

Output Gap

The rebound will be slower than usual because the slump was caused by a financial crisis and is synchronized around the world, the fund said. The report included a table which showed the so-called output gap, the excess of world supply over demand, will remain negative for the foreseeable future.

Advanced economies will continue to lead the slump by shrinking 3.8 percent this year and failing to grow in 2010, the IMF said. The fund cut its forecasts for this year and next for all the Group of Seven economies and said Germany, Italy and the U.K. will still be shrinking in 2010.

The U.S. economy will slide 2.8 percent this year before stalling next year and the euro area will contract 4.2 percent in 2009 and 0.4 percent in 2010, the report said. While Japanese gross domestic product will fall 6.2 percent this year, it will then rise 0.5 percent next year.

Speaking ahead of their April 24 meeting in Washington, finance ministers from G7 nations today said that even given signs of stabilization, their economies are still in trouble and that they would continue to pursue policies designed to restore growth.

U.S. Role

U.S. Treasury Secretary Timothy Geithner cited the IMF data as reason for officials "to strengthen the basis for recovery." Canadian Finance Minister Jim Flaherty said while he sees "small, encouraging signs" in the global economy, it remains "in the midst of" the crisis.

Blanchard said in a Bloomberg Television interview today that the United States will play a "major role" in determining when the global economy and key nations start turning around. "The rest of the world is not going to recover unless the U.S. recovers."

Policy makers were urged to "act decisively" and not delay their responses to the financial crisis.

Emerging and developing economies will grow 1.6 percent this year and 4 percent next year, reductions of 1.7 percentage point and 1 percentage point respectively from previous forecasts, the IMF said. They will suffer net capital outflows of more than 1 percent of GDP this year and only the highest-grade borrowers will be able to tap new funding.

The risk of corporate defaults in such economies is also "rising to dangerous levels," the IMF said.

China, India

Growth in China, where the IMF said there is scope for further easing of monetary and fiscal policy, is forecast to slow to 6.5 percent this year before climbing to 7.5 percent in 2010. India's economy will grow 4.5 percent in 2009 and 5.6 percent in 2010, compared with 7.3 percent last year.

While stopping short of predicting deflation, the fund said the risk was greater than during the last such scare earlier this decade. Consumer prices will drop 0.2 percent in advanced economies this year before rising 0.3 percent next year and there is a risk of a steeper initial decline, the IMF said.

Policy makers were urged to "act decisively" and not delay their responses to the financial crisis. Balance sheets should be revived by removing bad assets and injecting new capital, the IMF said.

Monetary and fiscal policies should be "geared as far as possible" to bolstering demand and where flexibility remains for more monetary stimulus, such as at the European Central Bank, it "should be used quickly," the fund said.

Measures' Impact

"In advanced economies, scope for easing monetary policy further should be used aggressively to counter deflation risks," the fund said, forecasting interest rates will remain near zero in major economies. Governments should not prematurely withdraw stimulus measures and perhaps add to them, it said.

At the briefing after the report was released, Blanchard said "strong" fiscal policies thus far have made a "gigantic difference," while urging governments to resist complacency.

"Things are not great, they could have been extremely bad," Blanchard said. "To the extent that more can be done, it should be done."

Exit strategies also should be outlined for when recovery takes hold, the fund said. "Acting too quickly would risk undercutting what is likely to be a fragile recovery, but acting too slowly could risk a return to overheating and new asset-price bubbles," it said.

Downside Risks

Risks to the outlook remain skewed to the downside and include the possibility that policies will fail to stop weakening economies and financial conditions from feeding on each other. "In a highly uncertain context, fiscal and monetary policies may fail to gain traction," the report said.

Meanwhile, the fund said confidence and spending could be revived faster than expected should investors endorse policy steps by authorities.

Global trade is forecast to plunge 11 percent this year after expanding 3.3 percent in 2008, undermining economies that rely on exports such as those of Germany and China, according to the report. The crisis has prompted a "flight to safety" which boosted the major currencies.

The current recession is the world's first since 1991 and the fourth since World War II.

The slowdown is hurting companies such as Caterpillar Inc., the world's largest maker of bulldozers and excavators, which yesterday posted its first quarterly net loss in 16 years as a result of the global recession.

Peoria, Illinois-based Caterpillar said it expects the world economy to decline about 1.3 percent this year. Chief Executive Officer Jim Owens has already cut more than 24,000 jobs since December.

Unemployment

Such cutbacks will propel unemployment to 9.2 percent next year in the advanced economies from 8.1 percent this year, while in the United States the jobless rate will jump to 10.1

percent in 2010, the IMF said. The Labor Department said this month that unemployment in the United States climbed to a 25-year high of 8.5 percent in March.

Yahoo! Inc., owner of the second-most popular U.S. Internet search engine, announced payroll cuts yesterday, citing a slowdown in online-advertisement sales. The company, based in Sunnyvale, California, said it will cut 5 percent of its workforce or 700 jobs.

The IMF also issued a new definition of a global recession based on a drop in real per capita world GDP alongside changes in industrial production, capital flows, trade, oil consumption and unemployment. Under this measure, the current recession is the world's first since 1991 and the fourth since World War II. The new interpretation supersedes a rule of thumb that declared a downturn when growth was less than 2.5 percent or 3 percent.

"It's going to be a while before a report is going to say there's clear signs of an economic recovery," said Colin Bradford, an economist at the Brookings Institution in Washington.

The U.S. Job Market Is No Longer in Free Fall

Gary Burtless

Gary Burtless is an economist and a senior fellow in economic studies at the Brookings Institution, where he researches labor market policy, income distribution, population aging, and similar economic issues.

Who would have thought one year ago [May 2008] that economists and investors would be celebrating a jobs report showing payroll employment fell "only" 540,000 in a month? But that seems to be the case. April's [2009] job loss of 540,000 looks pretty good when the monthly drop of payroll employment in the previous four months averaged 700,000. To be sure, the monthly drop in private sector jobs still looked awful in April. Part of the improvement in overall employment loss is explained by a big jump in federal government employment, much of it due to hiring for the 2010 Census. Even in the private sector, however, the pace of job loss slowed, reflecting a slower rate of employment shrinkage in both the goods-producing and service-producing sectors. It no longer looks as though the job market is in free fall. It is still in decline, but the decline is not accelerating. It may be slowing.

A Slower Layoff Rate

The April statistics on initial unemployment insurance (UI) claims also gave us a hint the layoff rate may have slowed. The percentage of UI-covered workers who are losing their jobs and filing a new UI claim fell modestly in April. Since reaching a peak near the end of March, the weekly new-layoff rate

Gary Burtless, "Have Job Losses Peaked?" *National Journal*, May 11, 2009. Reproduced by permission.

has fallen about 10%. Of course, the layoff rate remains terribly high. In April, slightly more than 2% of workers in UI-covered jobs filed a new claim for unemployment benefits. That's almost twice the new-layoff rate we experienced in 2007, before the current recession began.

The latest statistics on payroll employment and UI claims may be giving us a hint that, while the economy is still shrinking, the pace of decline is slowing.

Many people may be surprised to learn that the peak layoff rate in late March 2009 was only modestly higher than the peak rate in the early 1990s, and it was far below the peak rate we experienced in the 1981–1982 recession. People who were distressed by the record number of new claims for UI this past winter should bear in mind that the historical number of new UI claims can only be assessed relative to the number of workers who hold jobs that are covered by the unemployment insurance system. Because the U.S. population has grown, the number of UI-covered workers is much larger today than it was in the 1980s and early 1990s. The shockingly high number of people filing new UI claims last March must therefore be weighed against the much larger number of workers who are at risk of being laid off and filing a claim for benefits. Today's laid off workers might be a little less likely to file a claim for UI benefits than was the case for laid off workers back in 1982 or 1991, though it's hard to see why. Workers in many states can now obtain more than a year of UI benefits after they file a successful claim. The maximum permitted spell of UI compensation was shorter in the 1980s and 1990s. In addition, the 2009 federal stimulus package provided a boost in UI benefits of $25 a week, giving laid off workers an extra incentive to file a claim.

The payroll employment numbers and the unemployment insurance statistics gave us the first indicator we were heading into a recession last year. In the first half of 2008, when the GDP [gross domestic product, a measure of a country's total economic output] statistics still showed a growing economy, the employment and unemployment statistics provided clear signals of rising distress in the job market. The latest statistics on payroll employment and UI claims may be giving us a hint that, while the economy is still shrinking, the pace of decline is slowing. That's good news if you feared a recurrence of the Great Depression.

The Recession Appears to Be Lifting

Jeannine Aversa

Jeannine Aversa is a reporter for the Associated Press, an international news service.

Fresh signs emerged Monday [June 1, 2009] that the recession is letting up.

Manufacturing's slide is slowing. Builders are boosting spending on construction projects—including homes. And consumers aren't cutting back as much as some had feared.

A trio of reports gave Wall Street a big lift on the same day that industrial icon General Motors Corp. filed for bankruptcy protection. The federal government is taking a majority ownership stake in the company, which announced new plant closings.

Investors and economists focused instead on the encouraging news about the economy.

The Dow Jones Industrial Average [a stock market index] jumped 221 points, or 2.6 percent. And the Standard & Poor's 500 index and NASDAQ composite reached their highest levels this year.

"What looked like a flicker of light at the end of the tunnel is now starting to look like a beacon," said Richard Yamarone, economist at Argus Research. "We are no longer in the deep throes of recession. A recovery may be just a few months away."

A Trio of Reports

Economists were especially heartened by a report from the Institute for Supply Management that showed U.S. manufactur-

Jeannine Aversa, "Hopeful Signs for Economy Emerge in Latest Data," Yahoo! News/ The Associated Press, June 1, 2009. http://news.yahoo.com. Reprinted with permission of the Associated Press.

ing activity shrinking at a slower pace in May. Reports from Asia and Europe indicated similar improvements in their manufacturing sectors.

The institute's index came in at 42.8—its highest since September and up from 40.1 in April. A reading below 50 still indicates activity contracted, but the figure surpassed economists' forecasts.

Importantly, an index of new orders placed with U.S. factories rose to 51.1 in May. It was the first time this barometer had grown since November 2007, the month before the recession began.

And businesses' inventories shrank, suggesting supplies will soon need to be replenished. That would boost factory production, aiding overall economic activity.

"The data add to mounting evidence of an abatement in the deep factory-sector recession," said Cliff Waldman, economist at Manufacturers Alliance/MAPI, a manufacturing research group.

"The worst has clearly passed for U.S. factories," he said. "Nonetheless, a real recovery might be months away. The global economic picture remains difficult, and financial conditions are still problematic. But better days are clearly ahead."

Another report, from the Commerce Department, said construction spending rose a surprising 0.8 percent in April. Economists had been expecting a 1.2 percent decline.

It marked the second straight month that construction spending has risen. Before that, spending had fallen for five straight months. Private builders in April increased spending on housing projects—something that hadn't happened since August.

A third report showed consumers trimmed spending by 0.1 percent in April, slightly less than the 0.2 percent reduction economists were forecasting. Still, it marked the second straight month that consumers cut back, a reminder that many shoppers remain wary.

With unemployment rising, consumers are expected to stay fairly cautious in the months ahead. Because consumer spending accounts for roughly 70 percent of overall economic activity, it's closely watched by economists.

Americans' incomes—the fuel for future spending—jumped 0.5 percent in April, after two straight months of declines. The improvement was due to tax cuts and benefit payments flowing from President Barack Obama's stimulus package, the government noted. Wages and salaries were flat in April.

All three reports, though, reinforced analysts' beliefs that the economy isn't sinking nearly as much now as it was in the prior six months.

A Slow Recovery

Forecasters at the National Association for Business Economics, or NABE, predict the economy will contract at a 1.8 percent pace in the April–June quarter.

Other analysts think the economic decline could be steeper—around a 3 percent pace. Some think it could be less—about a 1 percent pace.

The expected improvement would come from less drastic spending cutbacks by businesses. And companies could start to rebuild razor-thin inventories.

In the first quarter, the economy contracted at a 5.7 percent pace. That followed a staggering 6.3 percent annualized drop in the fourth quarter of 2008—the biggest in a quarter-century.

Federal Reserve Chairman Ben Bernanke has said he's hopeful the recession will end later this year. And NABE forecasters say the economy could start growing again as early as the third quarter. Obama's stimulus package of increased government spending and tax cuts should fuel economic activity.

But Bernanke and other economists warn that the recovery will be slow, and unemployment will keep rising well after the recession has ended. Some predict it could hit 10.7 percent by the second quarter of next year.

The nation's unemployment rate jumped to 8.9 percent in April, the highest in 25 years. Economists estimate the rate climbed to 9.2 percent in May. The government releases the unemployment report on Friday [June 5, 2009].

Since the start of the recession in December 2007, the economy has lost 5.7 million jobs.

Against this backdrop, consumers are motivated to save more.

Americans' personal savings rate zoomed to 5.7 percent in April, the highest since February 1995. The level of savings—$620.2 billion—was the most on records dating to January 1959. All that reflects a more thrifty consumer whose wealth—notably nest eggs, investment holdings and home values—has been hard hit by the recession.

The U.S. Economy Will Gradually Rebound in the Future

Merle David Kellerhals Jr.

Merle David Kellerhals Jr. is a staff writer for America.gov, a government Web site run by the U.S. State Department.

While domestic unemployment is likely to increase in the coming months, there are indications that the pace of the U.S. economic crisis may be slowing, Federal Reserve Chairman Ben Bernanke says.

"Consumer spending, which dropped sharply in the second half of last year, grew in the first quarter," Bernanke said in congressional testimony May 5 [2009]. "In coming months, households' spending power will be boosted by the fiscal stimulus program, and we have seen some improvement in consumer sentiment."

Impact of the Recession

Since the recession began in December 2007, the real gross domestic product (GDP), the total value of U.S. goods and services produced in a year and a basic measure of an economy's performance, dropped at an annual rate of more than 6 percent in the fourth quarter of 2008 and the first quarter of this year, Bernanke said.

"Among the enormous costs of the downturn is the loss of some 5 million payroll jobs over the past 15 months," he said in prepared testimony for Congress's Joint Economic Committee. The most recent information from the labor market indicates the United States can expect sizeable job losses and increased unemployment in coming months.

Merle David Kellerhals Jr., "U.S. Economy Should Improve in Late 2009, Fed Chair Bernanke Says," America.gov, May 5, 2009. www.america.gov.

Bernanke said conditions in the labor market and declines in the value of housing along with tight consumer credit conditions will continue to hold consumers back from spending more until they experience a loosening of conditions that impact them directly. Contrasting to somewhat better news with consumers, Bernanke said the available indicators of business investment remain weak.

Economic activity abroad is ... an important consideration in how soon the U.S. economy rebounds.

There has been a 30 percent drop, at an annual rate, in the purchase of equipment and computer software by businesses in both the fourth quarter of 2008 and the first quarter of this year, he said. And the level of new orders for equipment remains below the level of shipments, which suggests a further near-term softness in business equipment spending, he said.

"Conditions in the commercial real estate sector are poor," Bernanke said. Adding to that bleak outlook is that credit conditions in commercial real estate are severely strained, with no commercial mortgage-backed securities having been issued in almost a year, he said.

Bernanke said economic activity abroad is also an important consideration in how soon the U.S. economy rebounds. "The steep drop in U.S. exports that began last fall has been a significant drag on domestic production, and any improvement on that front would be helpful," he said. "A few indicators suggest, again quite tentatively, that the decline in foreign economic activity may also be moderating."

Bernanke said inflation remains well under control as prices for energy and other essential commodities began falling rapidly in the second half of 2008. "Weakness in demand and reduced cost pressures have continued to keep inflation low so far this year," he said.

Economic Outlook

"We continue to expect economic activity to bottom out, then to turn up later this year," Bernanke testified.

Key to the economic turnaround is that the housing market is beginning to stabilize, and that the sharp inventory liquidation that has been occurring will slow over the next few quarters, he said.

The [economic] recovery will gain momentum only gradually and . . . economic slack will decline slowly.

But Bernanke warned that the forecast assumes the gradual repair of the financial system continues. "A relapse in financial conditions would be a significant drag on economic activity and could cause the incipient recovery to stall," he said.

Bernanke also said the recovery will gain momentum only gradually and that economic slack will decline slowly. And he said that businesses are likely to be cautious about hiring new workers, which means the unemployment rate could remain high for a time, even after economic growth returns. Normally, employment follows the economy, but does not lead it.

Inflation in this type of economic environment is expected to remain low, he said.

"A sustained recovery in economic activity depends critically on restoring stability to the financial system," he said. "However, financial markets and financial institutions remain under considerable stress, and cumulative declines in asset prices, tight credit conditions, and high levels of risk aversion continue to weigh on the economy."

CHAPTER 2

Are the Government's Anti-Recession Policies Working?

Chapter Preface

The heart of President Barack Obama's economic policies is the American Recovery and Reinvestment Act, a $787 billion economic stimulus package passed and signed into law in February 2009. The stimulus, which included tax cuts for ordinary Americans, infrastructure spending (such as highways and schools), and aid to states, was justified by the Obama administration as a measure that would boost government spending and jump-start the slow U.S. economy. President Obama explained that Americans, fearful about the recession, had dramatically cut back on their consumer spending, saving their money instead. However reasonable this human reaction is for individual families, Obama said, the aggregate effect on the whole economy is negative, reducing consumer demand and causing businesses to lay off employees and cut back on production—actions that only adversely affect a recession. The stimulus package, the Obama administration argued, would replace this lack of consumer spending with government spending, to create greater demand and stimulate businesses to hire and produce once again. President Obama has also sought to expand the money supply, by having the U.S. Federal Reserve—an independent federal agency that acts as the nation's central bank—lower interest rates and take other monetary actions.

Many commentators have described the Obama stimulus plan as pure Keynesian economics—a reference to economic theories developed by British economist John Maynard Keynes, which were publicized in the 1930s when the world was trying to recover from the Great Depression. Keynes's economic ideas were set forth in his 1936 book, *The General Theory of Employment, Interest and Money,* and were considered to be radical at the time. Keynes favored the idea that government spending should be used to boost the economy during a downturn. Before Keynes, most economists believed that economic markets should be self-regulating, but Keynes argued market-based economies could get stuck at a point where the private sector can no longer make necessary corrections, creating persistent high unemployment and stagnated growth. In these situations, Keynes believed that only large infusions of government stimulus could revive economic growth.

One way for government to stimulate a stuck economy is for the government to increase the money supply. Extra money in people's pockets, theoretically, encourages them to spend more, which in many cases will be enough to lift a sinking economy and restore the circular flow of money throughout the system. In the United States, the U.S. Federal Reserve Board is charged with this task of regulating monetary policy. The Federal Reserve, often called the Fed, can increase the money supply in several ways. First, the Fed can buy U.S. debt from commercial banks to increase the amounts they can lend. Second, the Fed can loosen credit requirements to increase the amount of money people can borrow. Another way is for the Fed to cut the prime lending rate—that is, the rate the Federal Reserve loans to commercial banks; this allows banks to reduce their interest rates on loans to individuals and businesses, spurring more economic activity.

Keynes approved of these monetary actions as a first step in combating recessions, but if monetary efforts do not work, Keynes believed that government should do what individuals are not doing—directly spend money to prime the pump of the economy—even if doing so required deficit spending, or spending more than the government was making from taxes and other income. According to Keynes, it doesn't really matter what the government spends the money on, because almost any type of spending will create jobs, but Keynes suggested that the best type of spending would be building homes, schools, infrastructure, or other projects that tangibly help people over the long run. A debate between conservatives and liberals continues, however, about whether Keynesian economic theories actually work.

Many liberal economists point to former president Franklin Roosevelt's New Deal programs as an example of Keynesian stimulus spending that worked to help end the Great Depression. Other commentators argue that it was the massive public spending for World War II that really cured the depression of the 1930s. Indeed, in about seven years of wartime spending, the United States went from the worst economic crisis ever known to the greatest economic boom in the nation's history. Notably, most economic experts consider both of these expenditures to be consistent with Keynes's theories, and the apparent success of the spending approach to the Great Depression caused governments all over the world to take a more active role in their economies. The authors of the viewpoints in the following chapter present some of the many opinions about whether the Obama administration's policies are working to end America's economic crisis.

The Government Is Responding to the Economic Crisis with Extraordinary Actions

Barack Obama

Barack Obama is the forty-fourth president of the United States.

It has now been twelve weeks since my administration began. And I think even our critics would agree that at the very least, we've been busy. In just under three months [since January 2009], we have responded to an extraordinary set of economic challenges with extraordinary action—action that has been unprecedented in both its scale and its speed. . . .

Our most urgent task has been to clear away the wreckage, repair the immediate damage to the economy, and do everything we can to prevent a larger collapse. And since the problems we face are all working off each other to feed a vicious economic downturn, we've had no choice but to attack all fronts of our economic crisis at once.

A Recovery Plan

The first step was to fight a severe shortage of demand in the economy. The Federal Reserve did this by dramatically lowering interest rates last year in order to boost investment. And my administration and Congress boosted demand by passing the largest recovery plan in our nation's history. It's a plan that is already in the process of saving or creating 3.5 million jobs over the next two years. It is putting money directly in people's pockets with a tax cut for 95% of working families that is now showing up in paychecks across America. And to

Barack Obama, "Remarks on the Economy, Georgetown University," The White House, Office of the Press Secretary, April 14, 2009.

cushion the blow of this recession, we also provided extended unemployment benefits and continued health care coverage to Americans who have lost their jobs through no fault of their own.

Now, some have argued that this recovery plan is a case of irresponsible government spending; that it is somehow to blame for our long-term deficit projections, and that the federal government should be cutting instead of increasing spending right now. So let me tackle this argument head on.

To begin with, economists on both the left and right agree that the last thing a government should do in the middle of a recession is to cut back on spending. You see, when this recession began, many families sat around their kitchen table and tried to figure out where they could cut back. So do many businesses. That is a completely responsible and understandable reaction. But if every family in America cuts back, then no one is spending any money, which means there are more layoffs, and the economy gets even worse. That's why the government has to step in and temporarily boost spending in order to stimulate demand. And that's exactly what we're doing right now.

The heart of this financial crisis is that too many banks and other financial institutions simply stopped lending money.

Second of all, I absolutely agree that our long-term deficit is a major problem that we have to fix. But the fact is that this recovery plan represents only a tiny fraction of that long-term deficit. As I will discuss in a moment, the key to dealing with our deficit and debt is to get a handle on out-of-control health care costs—not to stand idly by as the economy goes into free fall.

So the recovery plan has been the first step in confronting this economic crisis. The second step has been to heal our financial system so that credit is once again flowing to the businesses and families who rely on it.

Healing the Financial Crisis

The heart of this financial crisis is that too many banks and other financial institutions simply stopped lending money. In a climate of fear, banks were unable to replace their losses by raising new capital on their own, and they were unwilling to lend the money they did have because they were afraid that no one would pay it back. It is for this reason that the last administration used the Troubled Asset Relief Program, or TARP, to provide these banks with temporary financial assistance in order to get them lending again.

Now, I don't agree with some of the ways the TARP program was managed, but I do agree with the broader rationale that we must provide banks with the capital and the confidence necessary to start lending again. That is the purpose of the stress tests that will soon tell us how much additional capital will be needed to support lending at our largest banks. Ideally, these needs will be met by private investors. But where this is not possible, and banks require substantial additional resources from the government, we will hold accountable those responsible, force the necessary adjustments, provide the support to clean up their balance sheets, and assure the continuity of a strong, viable institution that can serve our people and our economy.

Of course, there are some who argue that the government should stand back and simply let these banks fail—especially since in many cases it was their bad decisions that helped create the crisis in the first place. But whether we like it or not, history has repeatedly shown that when nations do not take early and aggressive action to get credit flowing again, they have crises that last years and years instead of months and months—years of low growth, low job creation, and low investment that cost those nations far more than a course of bold, upfront action. And although there are a lot of Americans who understandably think that government money would be better spent going directly to families and businesses instead of banks—"where's our bailout?" they ask—the truth is that a dollar of capital in a bank can actually result in eight or ten dollars of loans to families and businesses, a multiplier effect that can ultimately lead to a faster pace of economic growth.

On the other hand, there have been some who don't dispute that we need to shore up the banking system, but suggest that we have been too timid in how we go about it. They say that the federal government should have already preemptively stepped in and taken over major financial institutions the way that the FDIC [Federal Deposit Insurance Corporation, a government agency that insures bank deposits] currently intervenes in smaller banks, and that our failure to do so is yet another example of Washington coddling Wall Street. So let me be clear—the reason we have not taken this step has nothing to do with any ideological or political judgment we've made about government involvement in banks, and it's certainly not because of any concern we have for the management and shareholders whose actions have helped cause this mess.

Rather, it is because we believe that preemptive government takeovers are likely to end up costing taxpayers even more in the end, and because it is more likely to undermine than to create confidence. Governments should practice the same principle as doctors: First do no harm. So rest assured—we will do whatever is necessary to get credit flowing again, but we will do so in ways that minimize risks to taxpayers and to the broader economy. To that end, in addition to the program to provide capital to the banks, we have launched a plan that will pair government resources with private investment in order to clear away the old loans and securities—the so-called toxic assets—that are also preventing our banks from lending money.

Now, what we've also learned during this crisis is that our banks aren't the only institutions affected by these toxic assets that are clogging the financial system. AIG [American International Group, an insurance corporation], for example, is not a bank. And yet because it chose to insure trillions of dollars worth of risky assets, its failure could threaten the entire financial system and freeze lending even further. This is why, as frustrating as it is—and I promise you, nobody is more frustrated than me—we've had to provide support for AIG. It's also why we need new legal authority so that we have the power to intervene in such financial institutions, just like a bankruptcy court does with businesses that hit hard times, so that we can restructure these businesses in an orderly way that does not induce panic—and can restructure inappropriate bonus contracts without creating a perception that government can just change compensation rules on a whim.

This is also why we're moving aggressively to unfreeze markets and jump-start lending outside the banking system, where more than half of all lending in America actually takes place. To do this, we've started a program that will increase guarantees for small business loans and unlock the market for auto loans and student loans. And to stabilize the housing market, we've launched a plan that will save up to four million responsible homeowners from foreclosure and help many millions more refinance.

Fixing the Auto Industry

In a few weeks, we will also reassess the state of Chrysler and General Motors [GM], two companies with an important place in our history and a large footprint in our economy—but two companies that have also fallen on hard times.

Late last year [December 2008], the companies were given transitional loans by the previous administration to tide them over as they worked to develop viable business plans. But the plans they developed fell short, and so we have given them some additional time to work these complex issues through. We owed that, not to the executives whose bad bets contributed to the weakening of their companies, but to the hundreds of thousands of workers whose livelihoods hang in the balance.

To coordinate a global response to this global recession, I went to the meeting of the G-20 nations in London.

It is our fervent hope that in the coming weeks, Chrysler will find a viable business partner and that GM will develop a business plan that will put it on a path to profitability without endless support from the American taxpayer. In the meantime, we are taking steps to spur demand for American cars and provide relief to autoworkers and their communities. And we will continue to reaffirm this nation's commitment to a 21st century American auto industry that creates new jobs and builds the fuel-efficient cars and trucks that will carry us toward a clean energy future.

A Global Response

Finally, to coordinate a global response to this global recession, I went to the meeting of the G-20 nations [a group of the world's most industrialized countries] in London the other week. Each nation has undertaken significant stimulus to spur demand. All agreed to pursue tougher regulatory reforms. We also agreed to triple the lending capacity of the International Monetary Fund, an international financial institution supported by all the major economies, and provide direct assistance to developing nations and vulnerable populations— because America's success depends on whether other nations have the ability to buy what we sell. We pledged to avoid the trade barriers and protectionism that hurts us all in the end. And we decided to meet again in the fall to gauge our progress and take additional steps if necessary.

So all of these actions—the Recovery Act, the bank capitalization program, the housing plan, the strengthening of the nonbank credit market, the auto plan, and our work at the G-20—have been necessary pieces of the recovery puzzle. They have been designed to increase aggregate demand, get credit flowing again to families and businesses, and help them ride out the storm. And taken together, these actions are starting to generate signs of economic progress. Because of our recovery plan, schools and police departments have cancelled planned layoffs. Clean energy companies and construction companies are rehiring workers to build everything from energy efficient windows to new roads and highways. Our housing plan has helped lead to a spike in the number of homeowners who are taking advantage of historically low mortgage rates by refinancing, which is like putting a $2,000 tax cut in your pocket. Our program to support the market for auto loans and student loans has started to unfreeze this market and securitize more of this lending in the last few weeks. And small businesses are seeing a jump in loan activity for the first time in months.

This is all welcome and encouraging news, but it does not mean that hard times are over. 2009 will continue to be a difficult year for America's economy. The severity of this recession will cause more job loss, more foreclosures, and more pain before it ends. The market will continue to rise and fall. Credit is still not flowing nearly as easily as it should. The process for restructuring AIG and the auto companies will involve difficult and sometimes unpopular choices. All of this means that there is much more work to be done. And all of this means that you can continue to expect an unrelenting, unyielding, day-by-day effort from this administration to fight for economic recovery on all fronts.

Preventing Another Recession

But even as we continue to clear away the wreckage and address the immediate crisis, it is my firm belief that our next task is to make sure such a crisis never happens again. Even as we clean up balance sheets and get credit flowing; even as people start spending and businesses start hiring—we have to realize that we cannot go back to the bubble and bust economy that led us to this point.

It is simply not sustainable to have a 21st century financial system that is governed by 20th century rules and regulations that allowed the recklessness of a few to threaten the entire economy. It is not sustainable to have an economy where in one year, 40% of our corporate profits came from a financial sector that was based too much on inflated home prices, maxed out credit cards, overleveraged banks and overvalued assets; or an economy where the incomes of the top 1% have skyrocketed while the typical working household has seen their income decline by nearly $2,000.

We cannot rebuild this economy on the same pile of sand. We must build our house upon a rock. We must lay a new foundation for growth and prosperity.

For even as too many were chasing ever-bigger bonuses and short-term profits over the last decade, we continued to neglect the long-term threats to our prosperity: the crushing burden that the rising cost of health care is placing on families and businesses; the failure of our education system to prepare our workers for a new age; the progress that other nations are making on clean energy industries and technologies while we remain addicted to foreign oil; the growing debt that we're passing on to our children. And even after we emerge from the current recession, these challenges will still represent major obstacles that stand in the way of our success in the 21st century.

There is a parable at the end of the Sermon on the Mount that tells the story of two men. The first built his house on a pile of sand, and it was destroyed as soon as the storm hit.

But the second is known as the wise man, for when "... the rain descended, and the floods came, and the winds blew, and beat upon that house ... it fell not: for it was founded upon a rock."

We cannot rebuild this economy on the same pile of sand. We must build our house upon a rock. We must lay a new foundation for growth and prosperity—a foundation that will move us from an era of borrow and spend to one where we save and invest; where we consume less at home and send more exports abroad.

It's a foundation built upon five pillars that will grow our economy and make this new century another American century: new rules for Wall Street that will reward drive and innovation; new investments in education that will make our workforce more skilled and competitive; new investments in renewable energy and technology that will create new jobs and industries; new investments in health care that will cut costs for families and businesses; and new savings in our federal budget that will bring down the debt for future generations. That is the new foundation we must build. That must be our future—and my administration's policies are designed to achieve that future.

The Federal Reserve's Monetary Policies Have Helped Prevent a Major Depression

Mike Whitney

Mike Whitney is a writer from Washington State who contributes regularly to Counterpunch, *an online magazine.*

Fed [Federal Reserve, the nation's central bank] chief Ben Bernanke's understanding of financial crises may have kept the country from sliding into another Great Depression. That doesn't mean that he's fixed the credit system, removed the nonperforming loans from the banks, or stopped housing prices from crashing. It simply means that pumping liquidity into the system—via huge increases in the money supply, zero-percent interest rates, and multi-trillion dollar lending facilities—has either slowed or reversed the rate of decline in many sectors of the economy. Monetary stimulus works. Manufacturing, industrial output, world trade and global stock markets had all been falling faster than during the Great Depression. Bernanke changed that. His aggressive monetary policy helped to stabilize the financial system and pull the economy back from the brink.

In April [2009], retail sales rose slightly as did consumer spending. The service industries contracted less than expected and manufacturing (ISM) showed modest gains. There are also signs that housing prices are flattening out although future price declines are still expected to be somewhere in the range of 10 to 20 percent. (Housing prices have already slipped 29 percent since their peak in 2006.) The underlying problems in the economy have not been fixed, but green shoots are popping up.

Mike Whitney, "Has Bernanke Pulled the Economy Back from the Brink?" *Counterpunch*, May 8–10, 2009. www.counterpunch.org. Reproduced by permission.

Wall Street has taken these first signs of recovery and turned them into an impressive 8-week rally. The S&P 500 has soared 35 percent in the last two months while the Dow is up nearly 30 percent. Traders have shrugged off grim earnings reports and myriad other distress signals and joined in the festivities. On CNBC, the financial channel, they're calling it the TARP [a reference to Troubled Asset Relief Program, a federal program to bail out failing banks] Rally. The $700 billion bank bailout bill is now credited with lifting the market out of the doldrums and sending stocks higher. It should be renamed the "Bernanke Rally"; without the Fed chief's quantitative easing and toxic asset lending programs the Dow would be languishing in the 6,000 range.

The underlying problems in the economy have not been fixed, but green shoots are popping up.

The Bank Problem

On the topic of the bank stress test results, [financial Web site] Bloomberg reports:

> The Federal Reserve determined that 10 U.S. banks need to raise a total of $74.6 billion in capital, a finding that Chairman Ben Bernanke said should reassure investors about the soundness of the financial system.

> The results showed that losses at the banks under 'more adverse' economic conditions than most economists anticipate could total $599.2 billion over two years. Mortgage losses present the biggest part of the risk, at $185.5 billion. Trading accounts were the second-largest vulnerability, with potential losses of $99.3 billion.

> Regulators have determined that Bank of America Corp. requires about $34 billion in new capital, the largest need among the 19 biggest U.S. banks subjected to stress tests,

said a person with knowledge of the matter. Bank of America fell 9 percent in trading before U.S. exchanges opened.

Citigroup's requirement for deeper reserves to offset potential losses over the coming two years is about $5 billion, people with knowledge of that bank's results said. Wells Fargo requires about $15 billion, while GMAC's need is $11.5 billion, one person said.

The stress tests are a public relations ploy designed to build confidence in the banking system and to fend off demands that insolvent banks be taken into conservatorship by the government. The market will decide whether [Timothy] Geithner's tests are credible or not; the jury is still out. Initial results indicate significantly smaller losses than estimates by the IMF [International Monetary Fund, an international lending organization] and the vast number of economists. So, who is right: Geithner or the IMF?

If Geithner is right—and the banks are in such great shape—then why is the taxpayer being asked to provide up to $2 trillion through the Term Asset-Backed Securities Loan Facility (TALF) and the Public-Private Investment Program (PPIP) to purchase the banks' garbage assets?

The [bank] stress tests are a public relations ploy designed to build confidence in the banking system.

Regardless of the stress tests, the banking system is underwater and the problems are not going away. The Treasury has given the failing banks 6 months to submit a plan of action for addressing their capital needs. It's a "win-win" situation for the banksters who believe that the recession will be over by then and their mortgage-backed securities will have regained much of their lost value. It's a pipe dream. More likely, unemployment and foreclosures will continue to rise through 2010, putting greater pressure on banks' balance sheets and forcing government intervention. The only alternative is raising capital from private lenders, but that will be a daunting task. The Saudis and China are no longer investing in failing US financial institutions. The capital faucet has been turned off. Obama will have to go to Congress for another multibillion dollar bailout.

According to author F. William Engdahl [in an April 2009 *Asia Times* article]:

> Five US banks, according to data in the just-released federal Office of the Comptroller of the Currency's Quarterly Report on Bank Trading and Derivatives Activities, hold 96 percent of all US bank derivatives positions in terms of nominal values, and an eye-popping 81 percent of the total net credit risk exposure in event of default.
>
> The top three are, in declining order of importance: JPMorgan Chase, which holds a staggering $88 trillion in derivatives; Bank of America with $38 trillion, and Citibank with $32 trillion. Number four in the derivatives sweepstakes is Goldman Sachs, with a mere $30 trillion in derivatives; number five, the merged Wells Fargo-Wachovia Bank, drops dramatically in size to $5 trillion. Number six, Britain's HSBC Bank USA, has $3.7 trillion.

The derivatives meltdown could have been avoided if [the] Glass-Steagall [Act] had not been repealed. Instead, the biggest banks have become the most reckless speculators creating trillions of dollars in poison assets, which will eventually be dumped [on] the taxpayer. Even worse, the banks have used their political influence to transform the FDIC [Federal Deposit Insurance Corporation] (the agency that guarantees bank deposits) into the primary funding mechanism for the purchase of toxic assets through the Treasury's Public-Private Investment Program (PPIP). Bernanke helped Geithner launch the PPIP and was part of the [Alan] Greenspan-led deregulatory movement which created the very problems he's now trying to resolve. Neither Bernanke nor Geithner have made any effort to restore the regulatory regime that preceded the crisis.

A Gloomy Situation

Bernanke made this gloomy statement to Congress on May 5:

> The U.S. economy has contracted sharply since last autumn, with real gross domestic product (GDP) [a measure of a country's total economic output] having dropped at an annual rate of more than 6 percent in the fourth quarter of 2008 and the first quarter of this year. Among the enormous costs of the downturn is the loss of some 5 million payroll jobs over the past 15 months. . . . We are likely to see further sizable job losses and increased unemployment in coming months. . . .
>
> A number of factors are likely to continue to weigh on consumer spending, among them the weak labor market and the declines in equity and housing wealth that households have experienced over the past two years. In addition, credit conditions for consumers remain tight. . . .
>
> The available indicators of business investment remain extremely weak. Spending for equipment and software fell at an annual rate of about 30 percent in both the fourth and first quarters, and the level of new orders remains below the level of shipments, suggesting further near-term softness in business equipment spending. . . . Surveyed firms are still reporting net declines in new orders and restrained capital spending plans. Our recent survey of bank loan officers reported further weakening of demand for commercial and industrial loans. The survey also showed that the net fraction of banks that tightened their business lending policies stayed elevated, although it has come down in the past two surveys.
>
> Conditions in the commercial real estate sector are poor. Vacancy rates for existing office, industrial, and retail proper-

ties have been rising, prices of these properties have been falling, and, consequently, the number of new projects in the pipeline has been shrinking.

We continue to expect economic activity to bottom out, then to turn up later this year.... An important caveat is that our forecast assumes continuing gradual repair of the financial system; a relapse in financial conditions would be a significant drag on economic activity and could cause the incipient recovery to stall.

Even after a recovery gets under way, the rate of growth of real economic activity is likely to remain below its longer-run potential for a while, implying that the current slack in resource utilization will increase further. We expect that the recovery will only gradually gain momentum and that economic slack will diminish slowly. In particular, businesses are likely to be cautious about hiring, implying that the unemployment rate could remain high for a time, even after economic growth resumes.

In this environment, we anticipate that inflation will remain low.

In other words, "The economy stinks and unemployment is going up. People have lost a bundle on their homes and they can count on losing even more. Business is slow, the banks aren't lending and demand has fallen off a cliff. Things might get better, but if we have another Lehman-type blowup, all bets are off. The recovery will be weak and high unemployment will persist into the foreseeable future, but at least inflation won't be a problem. We think. If there's a problem we hadn't anticipated; please call. Yours, Ben B."

The economy is now in a downward spiral. Tightening in the credit markets has made it harder for consumers to borrow or businesses to expand. Overextended financial institutions are forced to shed assets at fire-sale prices to meet margin calls from the banks. Asset deflation is ongoing with no end in sight. Price declines in housing have reached 30 percent already and are accelerating on the downside. Unemployment is at a 40-year high and headed higher. There are no jobs; home equity and retirement funds are shrinking and prospects for a quick recovery are nil.

The stock market surge doesn't help working people who get paid by the hour and don't have the extra money to bet on equities. They can't move numbers from one ledger to another and magically show a profit. They have to balance their checkbooks, show up on time. For these people—the bulk of working Americans—the future has never been grimmer and less certain. They're afraid for their jobs, their standard of living and their kids. They aren't covered under the bailout, don't have a powerful constituency, and the recovery probably won't include them. There are no green shoots for working stiffs.

Personal debt-to-income has skyrocketed in the last decade. The average American has never been so underwater. Troubles in the credit markets have forced banks to cut credit lines and tightened lending standards are further exacerbating the problem. Consumers have cut back on spending fearing that the recession will deepen or they'll lose their jobs. At the same time, homeowner equity is vanishing at a record pace, leaving millions on the brink of bankruptcy. An article in *Barron's* [a financial magazine] sums it up like this:

> The complacent reaction among the investment cognoscenti is that the credit markets are wildly oversold. More likely . . . it has something to do with the fact that "an overwhelming portion of some $8 trillion in mortgage debt (or 80 percent of the total) is teetering on the edge of, or in some state of, negative equity."

> As to the Fed's claim that the equity of homeowners as a group stands at 43 percent, she (Stephanie Pomboy [an economic forecaster]) points out that what the Fed neglects to tell you is that roughly a third of them have their houses

free and clear. Lo and behold, some basic arithmetic reveals that 67 percent of homeowners with mortgages have equity of less than 15%. That, Stephanie comments dryly, suggests the 'destruction priced into the credit markets hardly seems out of whack with potential reality.'

And while, thanks to 'transfer of toxic assets to taxpayers' and the magic of accounting legerdemain, the scarred financials to some significant extent may be spared further pain, the same can't be said for the nonfinancial sector. Little recognized, she insists, is how much the extraordinary gains in domestic nonfinancial profits from the low in 2001 to the peak in 2006—a stunning rise of 388 percent—owed to the housing bubble.

Those gigantic gains have been wiped out leaving the average homeowner with a mere 15 percent equity stake in his home. If prices continue to fall, the vast majority of homeowners will be at or near destitution. If the Fed's plan was to shift the nation's wealth from homeowners to the investor class via the housing bubble, [it] may have achieved [its] goal.

A Failure to Help Homeowners

The Obama administration has done little to help struggling homeowners even though the incidents of predatory lending are widespread and overwhelmingly directed at poor people of color. The *New York Times* lashed out at Obama for not pushing cram-down legislation through Congress even though he gave the bill lip service during his presidential campaign. From the *New York Times* editorial:

> The Obama administration sat by last week as 12 Senate Democrats joined 39 Senate Republicans to block a vote on an amendment that would have allowed bankruptcy judges to modify troubled mortgages.

> Senator Obama campaigned on the provision. And President Obama made its passage part of his anti-foreclosure

plan. It would have been a very useful prod to get lenders to rework bad loans rather than leaving the modification to a judge.

But when the time came to stand up to the banking lobbies and cajole yes votes from reluctant senators—the White House didn't. When the measure failed, there wasn't even a statement of regret.

Digging out of the current recession won't be easy.

It would have been easy for Obama to twist a few arms in the Senate and push through the legislation, but he didn't lift a finger. Instead, he's focused on expanding the war in Pakistan and pushing through his pay-your-own-way health care boondoggle. Obama's pattern of backing away from his campaign promises suggests that he'll cave in when the critical union organizing bill, the Employee Free Choice Act (EFCA) comes up for a vote. Obama, no friend of labor, will be AWOL [absent without leave] once again.

A Rush Road Ahead

Bernanke may have saved the country from another Great Depression, but he'll have a tough time putting the economy back on track. The Fed's ideological bias keeps it from addressing the root problem of flagging demand. What's needed are policy makers who understand that the endless debt-expansion is not sustainable, and that maintaining a healthy economy requires higher wages and a narrowing of the income gap. Inequality leads to falling demand and boom-and-bust cycles. Fiscal stimulus can take up the slack in demand on a temporary basis, but eventually, wages and compensation need to be increased to rebalance the system. The economist James K. Galbraith made these observations on the state of affairs in a recent interview with the *Texas Observer*:

As a matter of economics, public spending substitutes for private spending. It provides jobs, motivates useful activity, staves off despair. But it is not self-sustaining in the absence of a viable private credit system. The idea that we will be on the road to full recovery and returning to high employment in a year or so therefore seems to me to be an illusion. And for this reason, the emphasis on short-term, 'shovel-ready' projects in the expansion package, while understandable, was a mistake. As in the New Deal [an economic recovery program during the 1930s], we need both the Works Progress Administration, headed by Harry Hopkins, to provide employment, and the Public Works Administration, headed by Harold Ickes, to rebuild the country.

The desire for a return to normal is very powerful. It motivates both the ritual confidence of public officials and the dry numerical optimism of business economists, who always see prosperity just around the corner. The forecasts of these people, like those of official agencies such as the Congressional Budget Office, always see a turnaround within a year and a return to high employment within four or five years. In a strict sense, the belief is without foundation. Liquidation of excessive debt is now, and will remain for a time, the highest priority of American households. That is in part because for the moment they want to hold on to cash, and therefore they do not wish to borrow, and in part because with the collapse of house values, they no longer have collateral to borrow against. And so long as that is the case, there can be no strong recovery of private spending or business investment.

Digging out of the current recession won't be easy. The wholesale credit system will have to be rebuilt, just as the financial system will have to be reregulated and reset at a lower level of economic activity. That means higher unemployment, smaller GDP, and falling demand. Debts will have to be written down or paid off. Deleveraging takes time. The fireworks in the stock market are premature. Recovery is still a long way off.

Most Americans Are Confident of President Obama's Ability to Respond to the Economic Crisis

Frank Newport

Frank Newport is editor in chief of Gallup.com and a vice president of Gallup, a polling organization based in New Jersey.

Over two-thirds of Americans—71%—have a great deal or a fair amount of confidence in President [Barack] Obama to do or recommend the right thing for the economy, a much higher level of confidence than is given to Federal Reserve Chairman Ben Bernanke, Treasury Secretary Tim Geithner, or the Democratic or Republican leaders in Congress.

These results, from a new April 6–9 [2009] Gallup poll, show that President Obama continues to be the individual upon whom Americans are most willing to bestow their confidence when it comes to the economy.

Poll Details

Americans' confidence in Obama on the economy is roughly similar to the confidence rating the public gave to President George W. Bush in April 2001, then in his initial quarter of governing, as is the case now for Obama. Obama gets slightly higher "a great deal of confidence" ratings than did Bush, while Bush received a slightly higher "fair amount" rating. In 2002 and 2003, Bush's ratings were similar to Obama's now. By April of 2008, his last year in office, Bush's overall confidence ratings on the economy had dropped to just 34%. . . .

Frank Newport, "Americans Most Confident in Obama on Economy: Democratic Leaders in Congress Fare Better than Republican Leaders," Gallup.com, April 13, 2009. www.gallup.com. Reproduced by permission.

As previous Gallup research has shown, Obama inspires significantly higher confidence than does Geithner, his Treasury secretary. Federal Reserve Chairman Bernanke has been instrumental in pushing through dramatic economic policies and changes in an effort to stimulate the economy, and Americans accord him about the same level of confidence as they give to Geithner—but again, lower than the public's confidence in Obama.

Americans are not overwhelmingly positive about either the Democratic or the Republican leaders in Congress.

Bernanke was sworn in as chairman of the Federal Reserve in early 2006, under the Republican administration of George W. Bush. Bernanke's current confidence ratings are quite similar to where they have been over the last three years, despite the upheaval in the nation's economy in the last year.

It is unlikely that many Americans have a highly sophisticated understanding of the complex economic policies enacted in the last several months by either Bernanke or Geithner. Yet only 17% and 14% of Americans, respectively, are not able or willing to give an opinion on confidence in these two men's actions on the economy.

Americans are not overwhelmingly positive about either the Democratic or the Republican leaders in Congress. Still, the Democrats fare better on a comparative basis. Fifty-one percent of Americans have a great deal or a fair amount of confidence in the Democratic leaders, compared to 38% in the Republican leaders.

There are interesting differences in confidence levels in these individuals and leaders by partisan orientation.

- Obama gets almost universal confidence from Democrats, two-thirds support from independents, and just over one-third confidence from Republicans.

- Geithner appears to be somewhat more politicized than Bernanke. Geithner's confidence rating ranges from 70% among Democrats to just 24% among Republicans. Bernanke, on the other hand, has a more modest 28-point partisan gap, with a 64% confidence rating among Democrats vs. 36% among Republicans.

- The partisan ratings of Bernanke have shifted from last year, when he was serving under a Republican president. At that time, the Fed chairman received a 61% confidence rating from Republicans, 43% from independents, and just a 40% rating from Democrats. Apparently, Americans associate the Fed chairman with the particular president he happens to be serving under.

- Democrats have more faith in their leaders than Republicans do in theirs. Seventy-nine percent of Democrats say they have confidence in the Democratic leaders in Congress on the economy. Although this is lower than the confidence Democrats have in Obama, it is higher than the 57% confidence rating Republicans give the Republican leaders in Congress.

Survey Methods

Results are based on telephone interviews with 1,027 national adults, aged 18 and older, conducted April 6–9, 2009. For results based on the total sample of national adults, one can say with 95% confidence that the maximum margin of sampling error is ±3 percentage points.

President Obama's Economic Policies Are Delaying Economic Recovery

Peter Ferrara

Peter Ferrara is director of budget and entitlement policy at the Institute for Policy Innovation. He served in the White House Office of Policy Development under former president Ronald Reagan.

B y now, the current recession is officially the longest since World War II. The National Bureau of Economic Research dates the recession as starting some time during December 2007. The longest recession since World War II was 16 months, with the average being 10 months. By today, the current recession has clearly lasted more than 16 months.

Which raises the question, are President [Barack] Obama's economic policies promoting recovery, or delaying it? Why is this the longest recession since World War II? That is a period of almost 65 years! Would other economic policies better promote economic growth?

> *Even with [the recent stock market] . . . rebound, the market is still down 40% from its highs.*

Still No Recovery

Yes, there are signs that the economy is finally struggling out of its torpor. But the point is that the recovery is now officially overdue. It shouldn't just be showing signs of recovery. A full recovery should now be in full swing, given the historical record of the *last 65 years!*

Moreover, the signs of recovery are on Wall Street. But Main Street is still plunging deeper and deeper. Unemployment now at 8.5% will probably jump to close to 9% in Friday's [May 9, 2009] report, the highest in almost 30 years. Unemployment in the urban areas that supported Obama so heavily is now in double digits. In New York City, the black unemployment rate for men is near 50%.

We are still losing over 600,000 jobs a month. In his press conference on April 29, Obama stated that his stimulus package passed in February "has already saved or created over 150,000 jobs." But this number is completely made up. Since the beginning of the year, employment is down by 2.5 million jobs. Obama's statement is not evidence that his economic recovery plan is working. It is evidence that the president suffers from mental delusion.

But even Wall Street is not doing that well. People are cheered because the stock market has reversed a decline that seemed to be heading toward zero under the weight of Obama's new neo-socialism. But even with that rebound, the market is still down 40% from its highs.

Obama's economic policies are focused on attacking savings, investment, capital, and property rights.

The testimony of Federal Reserve [the national central bank, in charge of monetary policy] Chairman Ben Bernanke yesterday [May 5, 2009] did point to eventual recovery, but even he said,

> [T]he available indicators of business investment remain extremely weak. Spending for equipment and software fell at an annual rate of about 30 percent in both the fourth and first quarters, and the level of new orders remains below the level of shipments, suggesting further near-term softness in business equipment spending. Recent business surveys have been a bit more positive, but surveyed firms are still report-

ing net declines in new orders and restrained capital spending plans. Our recent survey of bank loan officers reported further weakening of demand for commercial and industrial loans. The survey also showed that the net fraction of banks that tightened their business lending policies stayed elevated, although it has come down in the past two surveys. Conditions in the commercial real estate sector are poor. Vacancy rates for existing office, industrial, and retail properties have been rising, prices of these properties have been falling, and, consequently, the number of new projects in the pipeline has been shrinking. Credit conditions in the commercial real estate sector are still severely strained, with no commercial mortgage-backed securities (CMBS) having been issued in almost a year.

Savings and Investment No, Capital Flight Yes

Indeed, Bernanke here inadvertently identifies the fundamental weakness in Obamanomics. *There is nothing anywhere in Obama's economic recovery plan to promote savings and investment. To the contrary, Obama's economic policies are focused on attacking savings, investment, capital, and property rights.* That is deliberate, because Obama ideologically sees savings, investment, capital, and property rights as the preserve of the rich, which he opposes, and, indeed, which he actually wants to *displace* with big government.

Even though American companies suffer the huge international competitive disadvantage of the second highest corporate tax rates in the industrialized world, Obama continues to scorn doing anything about this as taking us "back to the failed ideas of the past." On Monday, Obama was out promoting still more tax *increases* on corporate America. He foolishly thinks that imposing taxes on the overseas investments of American companies will force investment back to the USA. But this is just one more whupping stick in Obama's arsenal that is going to create full-scale capital flight from the United

States before his term is over. Watch as alert, independent thinking executives start to transform American companies with investments overseas into foreign companies with tentative investments in America at least for now.

[The Obama] stimulus package will create or save exactly zero jobs.

Obama's Hopeless Economics

Obama and his intellectual Minnie Mice defending his policies in think tanks, on the Internet, and on TV are expressly arguing that the way to promote economic growth is by massively increasing welfare, federal spending, federal deficits, and the national debt, to record levels, along with *higher* tax rates and *more costly* regulatory burdens. Does this sound like a promising strategy for economic growth to you? If so, you can best help your country by strictly devoting yourself to gardening, and avoiding all forms of political participation.

This is what Obama's ballyhooed stimulus package was all about. But readers of this column already know that borrowing a trillion dollars out of the private economy to put a trillion dollars of government spending back in does nothing to promote the economy on net. In particular, it does nothing to improve the incentives that govern economic growth. That is why this stimulus package will create or save exactly zero jobs.

This is also exactly what the Obama budget is all about. That budget proposed to increase federal spending for this year [2009] by an eardrum popping 34%, to a record total of $4 trillion, the highest ever. The deficit in the budget the Democrats adopted for this year is an extremist $1.7 trillion, more than 7 times [former president Ronald] Reagan's highest deficit of $221 billion, which caused so much howling among liberals and Democrats. By the tenth year under this Obama/Democrat budget policy, the deficit is still over $1 trillion. The deficit in the last budget adopted by a Republican-controlled Congress, in 2006 for fiscal year 2007, was $162 billion, less than *one-tenth* as much as this year's deficit!

Under Obama's budget, as a result, the national debt doubles after 5 years, and triples after 10, soaring as a percent of GDP [gross domestic product, a measure of a country's total economic output] from 40% today to a record-setting, neo-socialist 82%.

In his speech on the economy given at Georgetown University on April 14 [2009], Obama said, "We cannot rebuild this economy on the same pile of sand. We must build our house upon a rock. We must lay a new foundation for growth and prosperity, a foundation that will move us from an era of borrow and spend to one where we save and invest." Do the Obama stimulus package and budget plan look like they are trying to rebuild the economy upon a rock, or on the same pile of sand, a pile of extreme deficits and debt, government spending and welfare? Do they look like they are moving us "from an era of borrow and spend to one where we save and invest"? Where is anything in Obama's economic policies that will promote savings and investment? Isn't this statement just further evidence that Obama is delusional, and not living in the real world?

Even Obama's tax cut for 95% of Americans is not pro-growth. It is just a $400 per worker income tax *credit*, less than $8 per week, which is economically the same as sending each worker a $400 check. Borrowing $400 from someone else to give you $400 does not add anything to the economy on net. Going forward you still face the exact same economic incentives as before. For a tax cut to stimulate the economy, it must reduce tax *rates*, which strengthens incentives by allowing producers to keep a higher percentage of what they produce. This is what all of Reagan's tax cuts did, which is why they were so successful.

Moreover, the party-controlled mainstream media is cooperating in a huge cover-up of the fact that the budget adopted by the Democrat-controlled Congress does not include Obama's tax cut for 95% of Americans, the $400 per worker income tax credit, for more than 2 years. Obama won the election by promising over and over that he would cut taxes for 95% of Americans, and now in 18 months that will be gone.

Obama's Delusions

But Obama and congressional Democrats are continuing with their plan for a massive new tax by enacting their cap-and-trade anti–global warming scheme, imposing probably close to $2 trillion in increased costs on the U.S. economy. Consumers will pay for this through increased costs for electricity, gasoline, home heating oil, food, and any product that uses energy. This added burden will ultimately chase remaining manufacturing out of the country, sharply reduce America's standard of living, and tumble the American economy into long-term decline.

Obama, however, is actually arguing that imposing these massive new cap-and-trade costs on the economy will promote long-term economic growth. In his April 14 speech at Georgetown, Obama said,

> Now the third pillar in this new foundation [for economic growth] is to harness the renewable energy that can create millions of jobs in new industries. . . . The only way that we can truly spark the transformation that's needed is through a gradual, market-based cap on carbon pollution so that clean energy is the profitable kind of energy. . . . If businesses and entrepreneurs know today we're closing this carbon pollution loophole, they'll start investing in clean energy now and we'll see more companies constructing solar panels and workers building wind turbines and car companies manufacturing fuel-efficient cars and investors will put

money into a new energy technology and a small business will open to start selling it. That's how we can grow this economy, enhance our security and protect our planet at the same time.

So dumping $2 trillion in new costs on the economy will actually promote economic growth, because the added costs on suppliers of the proven energy sources that fuel our economy today will enable producers of the much more expensive, alternative, flower power, energy sources, based on sunbeams, the winds, and grass, to compete. No consideration in this vision for the jobs lost because energy costs in this new economy will be so much higher, or because energy supplies based on sunbeams, winds, and grass will be unreliable, or because the coal industry and other producers of traditional energy will be driven out of business. Again, is Obama mentally delusional?

And I haven't even gotten yet to Obama's tax *rate increases*, which will become effective at the end of next year [2010]. Top individual income tax rates will increase 20%, tax rates on capital gains and dividends will each rise 33%, and the death tax rate will be permanently restored at 45%. The expectation of these prospective tax rate increases will soon start *depressing* the economy, because incentives will be worsened.

Obama's shenanigans in trying to intimidate the senior bondholders in GM [General Motors] and Chrysler to give up their contractual rights to be paid first in favor of the more junior claims of the unions is also not helping. This will only discourage corporate lending from investors at home and abroad, and contribute to future capital flight. The auto bailouts will also be a continuing drain on the taxpayers, and hence the economy.

So, yes, I think Obama's hopeless economic policies are delaying rather than helping the economy. This is not to say that some economic recovery will not start later this year. I expect some growth to start by this summer only because the recession has gone on too long now, and this is still a fundamentally strong capitalist economy, for now. But this will be in spite of Obamanomics, not because of it.

Moreover, because of Obamanomics, I expect the growth to be relatively weak. I expect unemployment to remain persistently high, and in 2010 interest rates to rise, with renewed inflation then or by 2011 at the latest. I expect higher energy prices around then too, and an energy shortage and another recession in 2011. The expectation of future tax increases can cause higher growth this year, as people scramble to earn income now before tax rates rise, producing a more rapidly increasing stock market, which looks just 6 months ahead. But I expect another serious stock market reversal starting next year.

Gingrich's Better Alternative

[Former speaker of the House] Newt Gingrich has proposed a far more promising, 12-point, alternative economic recovery plan that should receive more attention. Gingrich recognizes that America's high corporate tax rates, close to 40% counting federal and state levies, leave American companies at an enormous competitive disadvantage. The EU [European Union] has reduced their average corporate tax rate from 38% to 24%. Germany and Canada have reduced their corporate tax rate to 19%, with Canada's going to 15%. India and China have lower corporate tax rates as well.

Gingrich would lower the 35% federal corporate tax rate to the 12.5% rate adopted by Ireland 20 years ago, which raised that long poor country from the second lowest per capita income in the EU to the second highest. Our own Treasury Department calculates that Ireland raises more corporate tax revenue as a percent of GDP with this 12.5% rate than we do with our 35% federal rate.

Gingrich would also reduce the 25% income tax rate paid by middle-class families to 15%, which would create an effective 15% flat tax for 90% of Americans. He would abolish the capital gains tax and the death tax, both of which involve double taxation of savings and investment. He would reduce spending to balance the budget, as he led Congress to do in the 1990s. He would also remove regulatory restrictions to allow production of more oil, natural gas, nuclear power, and alternative energy sources, providing reliable, low-cost energy supplies to power the American economy. This is a prescription for another economic boom.

President Obama's Stimulus Package May Eventually Cause Another Recession

Martin Hutchinson

Martin Hutchinson is an investment banker, a leading expert on the international financial markets, and a contributing editor to Money Morning, a financial Web site.

Could the massive Obama stimulus plan end up hurting the U.S. economy?

It's long been a worry, and now it's beginning to seem possible.

The latest housing reports suggest that the recent rapid run-up in 10-year Treasury bond yields may be having an unhealthy effect on the U.S. housing market. That tells me that—although home prices are back to their long-term average in terms of earnings—we may not yet be close to the price bottom.

If that's true, it's very bad news. A further substantial decline in housing prices would destabilize the U.S. banking system again, because of all the mortgage debt in it, which would cause a very nasty "second leg" economic downturn. That would have one very ironic further implication: U.S. president Barack Obama's $787 billion stimulus package—intended to help the U.S. economy push back the recession—would instead have succeeded in pushing it deeper into the mire.

A Jump in Interest Rate

A month ago [April 2009], it appeared that the housing market might be in the process of bottoming out. The ratio of house prices to average incomes—which peaked at about 4.5

to 1 in 2006—had fallen 33% from that apex, which brought the ratio close to its long-term average of 3.2 to 1, according to an S&P/Case-Shiller index [a source of home price data] report. While interest rates remained low and government-backed home financing was readily available, it appeared the forces pushing up house prices (low interest rates and accessible financing) might soon come into balance and then dominate the forces that push home prices down (an inventory overage).

The jump in interest rates—from 2.07% on the 10-year Treasury bond in December [2008] to around 3.65% today [May 29, 2009]—has weakened the case for a stabilization of housing prices. Mortgage rates, which were far below their levels of the last 30 years, have moved back above 5%—even for "conforming" mortgages. Thus, the Mortgage Bankers Association index of new mortgage applications was down 15% in the latest week. Meanwhile, new home sales have merely stabilized at very low levels of an annual rate around 350,000—compared to more than 2.0 million at the peak of the market, while the latest price statistics suggest that price declines continued to be quite rapid in March, and possibly even accelerated slightly.

This interest-rate increase does not currently seem to be caused by expectations of inflation, which has remained around 2% annually, although oil, gold and other commodity prices have ticked up. Instead, it seems to have been caused by the exceptionally high demands being made on the government bond market by the U.S. federal deficit, which is expected to total about 13% of gross domestic product (GDP), or more than $1.8 trillion, this year.

It's not surprising that such a blip should have occurred this month; federal tax receipts are at their peak in April, as companies and individuals pay their taxes due, so the beginning of May saw a resumption of mammoth U.S. Treasury funding needs after a month's pause.

Effects of Rising Interest Rates

If interest rates continue to increase, the effect on the already-weak housing market could be severe, as housing "affordability" would be reduced in a period in which prices were declining and unemployment was rising. That, in turn, could have a self-reinforcing downward effect on prices, as home inventories bloat further, and buyers hold back.

If interest rates keep rising, the effect of further housing-sector weakness and the wobbling banking system would overwhelm any stimulus benefits.

Currently, according to the S&P/Case-Shiller 20-city house price index, prices are down 32% from their peak, but remain 40% above 2000 levels, while consumer prices are only 24% above those of 2000. However, 2000 was not a "bear-market" year; prices had already enjoyed several years of rapid recovery from their early-1990s low. Should rising interest rates cause prices to continue falling to 2000's level (another 28% decline), then on average every 80% mortgage undertaken since May 2002 (when the index first went above 125% of 2000's level) would be underwater, having an owed principal amount that exceeds the actual current market value of the house. That would cause a surge in mortgage defaults more severe than any yet seen, extending far into the prime mortgage category—and probably causing the U.S. banking system to implode once again.

The stimulus-package funds, which began flowing in April, may actually induce some GDP growth this quarter. At the very least, the Obama administration infusion should hold the economy to a very minimal decline in GDP.

However, if interest rates keep rising, the effect of further housing-sector weakness and the wobbling banking system would overwhelm any stimulus benefits, and would cause a second "dip" in this recession—one that's far worse than the first. The stimulus would, in that event, have proved counter-productive, killing the very economic recovery it was supposed to have stimulated.

Rising interest rates will have adverse effects on all countries with large budget deficits, the most notable of which are Britain and Japan. The effects would be harsh enough to actually prevent those countries from recovering from their own recessions.

For investors, the remedy is clear: Look to invest in countries that have produced only modest stimulus packages, and whose budget deficits are currently the smallest. In the invaluable statistical section of the *Economist*, a number of countries are projected to have budget deficits of less than 3% of GDP in 2009, in spite of their recessions.

At that level, deficits are easy to finance, and do not force up interest rates, so economic recovery should be relatively rapid.

Even if There Is an Economic Revival, Long-Term Economic Problems Remain

Lee Sustar

Lee Sustar is an economics writer for SocialistWorker.org, a Web site published by the International Socialist Organization.

With unemployment reaching a new quarter-century high, the pressure is on for the [Barack] Obama administration to deliver help for working people and get the economy on the road to recovery. SocialistWorker.org economics writer Lee Sustar answers your questions about what Obama is proposing, and what the chances of success are.

Just when there was a discussion of a possible economic recovery, the government's report showed unemployment rising to 8.5 percent and another 650,000 jobs gone. Has the economy bottomed out?

No one really knows. Those who say that the worst is behind us either represent financial institutions trying to sell investments, or they're members of the Obama administration's economic team. Christina Romer, the chair of the White House Council of Economic Advisers, said recently that she's "incredibly confident" the U.S. economy will recover within a year.

It's true that job loss statistics released April 3 [2009], weren't as terrible as some economists were predicting. But they're plenty bad: The unemployment rate jumped from 8.1 to 8.5 percent. That figure rises to 15.6 percent when it includes "marginally attached workers"—those who've given up looking for work, or who've had to accept part-time work if they can't get a full-time job.

Lee Sustar, "Can Obama's Policies Fix the Economy?" SocialistWorker.org, April 8, 2009. www.socialistworker.org. Reproduced by permission.

Some economists anticipate that this broader measure of unemployment could surpass 18 percent in the months ahead. As the *Wall Street Journal* reported, "For people in this group, comparisons to the Great Depression (when 25 percent of Americans were out of work) may not look so wild, even if overall economic activity is holding up better."

[President Obama's economic strategy] constitutes the greatest government intervention in the economy since the Great Depression of the 1930s.

Can President Obama's economic policies counteract the economy's decline?

The Obama administration's strategy to revive the economy has four interrelated aspects: (1) shore up the private financial system by having the government absorb the banks' toxic assets and providing virtually free credit to corporate America; (2) revive consumer demand through tax cuts and easier terms for loans, including mortgages; (3) encourage the private sector to preserve or create jobs through stimulus spending and increases in the federal government's budget; and (4) force the restructuring of major industries, like auto, by attaching strict conditions on government loans.

All this constitutes the greatest government intervention in the economy since the Great Depression of the 1930s. Enormous economic powers are being concentrated in the executive branch of government via the U.S. Treasury and the Federal Reserve Bank, which is nominally independent, but in practice subordinate to the White House.

Paradoxically, however, the government is doing its utmost to leave private capitalists in control of financial institutions and government-financed companies, rather than nationalize them outright.

To be sure, the Obama administration forced Rick Wagoner to step down as CEO of General Motors to try and defuse anger over the $165 million bonuses paid to AIG executives [the American International Group, a giant insurer, which received billions of dollars in a federal bailout]. The government may also oust individual Wall Street bosses in the future if the pressure is sufficient.

Yet the Obama administration desperately wants to preserve private property, even when the companies involved couldn't survive without a constant infusion of taxpayer money.

Why not just nationalize the banks and other financial firms, rather than keep spending endless amounts of taxpayer money to keep them going—like the $173 billion given to AIG so far?

Defending private property is the default setting of U.S. politics. Nationalization, we're told, is for Europeans and third world leftists like Hugo Chávez of Venezuela.

But the more important factor is that the bankers have, in the words of economist Simon Johnson, carried out a "silent coup"—they've used their influence in Washington to block any attempt to make them politically accountable, let alone see their companies placed under government ownership.

Johnson should know what he's talking about. He's the former chief economist of the International Monetary Fund (IMF) [an international lending organization], a job that involved dictating the terms of financial restructuring in several countries. Now, he says, the U.S. financial barons are behaving just like the entrenched business oligarchs in countries like Russia and Indonesia.

So instead of the U.S. government taking over the banks, the bankers have taken even greater control of government policy. Treasury Secretary Tim Geithner, for example, was formerly president of the Federal Reserve Bank of New York. That is, Geithner was the main government overseer of Wall Street even as the big banks drove the economy off the cliff by loading up on mortgage-backed securities and complicated assets known as derivatives.

It was Geithner who negotiated the nationalization of AIG in a meeting that included Lloyd Blankfein, CEO of Goldman Sachs, a major trading partner with AIG. Is it a coincidence that Goldman recently collected $12.9 billion in payment from AIG—or rather, from the U.S. taxpayers, since our money only paused briefly on AIG's books before being funneled into the most powerful company on Wall Street?

But the AIG rip-off is only the beginning of the government's stupendous transfer of wealth from the working class to finance capital. Under Geithner's bank bailout program—the Public-Private Investment Program, or PPIP—the government will match private investors' initial investment in mortgages and other toxic assets.

The Federal Deposit Insurance Corp. (FDIC), the government agency that guarantees your checking or savings account, will be pressed into service for the PPIP. Under Geithner's plan, the FDIC will finance up to 85 percent of the money that hedge funds and other firms will use to buy those assets. (This legally dubious maneuver allows Geithner to come up with money for the program without going to Congress.)

In reality, the big banks remain crippled by bad investments and are using [government] . . . money to cover current and future losses.

If PPIP investments in toxic assets pay off, the government and private investors split the profits. Yet since private investors are required to put up so little of their own money, their gains could be as high as 30 percent. If the assets turn out to be bad, though, the government guarantees investors against losses.

Geithner somehow keeps a straight face when he claims that PPIP will help revive the economy. By assisting Wall Street, the cliché goes, the government will help Main Street through a revival in lending.

In reality, the big banks remain crippled by bad investments and are using the money to cover current and future losses. Even so, with commercial real estate tanking and corporate bankruptcies in the offing, things are likely to get worse for the banks before they get better.

That's why Wall Street was so anxious to get details of Geithner's PPIP. The real aim of the operation is for the government to absorb as much of the banks' losses as politically possible—which means workers will pay the price through higher taxes. In other words, Wall Street has gotten everything it wanted from Geithner, and then some.

And if any more proof is needed between the interpenetration of Wall Street and Washington, consider the career—and income—of Larry Summers, Obama's top economic adviser. A former Treasury secretary who was later forced out as president of Harvard for making sexist comments, Summers earned $5.2 million as a managing director of D.E. Shaw, a $30 billion hedge fund. He got another $2.77 million for speaking engagements, including $135,000 from Goldman Sachs.

Can Obama's economic policies work?

That depends on your definition of "work." Then there's the question, "Work for whom?"

First, the $787 [billion] stimulus package will give a modest boost to the U.S. economy. But every serious economist says this amount is too small to compensate for what the Congressional Budget Office estimates will be a $2 trillion shortfall in the U.S. economy over the next two years.

Obama's $3.6 trillion budget for fiscal 2010, which relies heavily on deficit spending, should provide some further lift to the economy—provided that Congress fully appropriates the money later this year.

Even so, the administration's biggest effort to juice the economy may come from the Federal Reserve [the nation's leading bank, in charge of monetary policy], which effectively created about $1.3 trillion out of thin air in order to purchase Treasury bonds and securities issued by the government-run mortgage companies, Fannie Mae and Freddie Mac.

By injecting this amount of money into the system while keeping interest rates near zero, the Fed aims to spur lending and economic activity in general.

The Fed is also set to finance another $1 trillion loan program, known as the Term Asset-Backed Securities Loan Facility (TALF). Under this program, the Fed will allow banks and other financial institutions to put up bad mortgage-backed securities and other toxic assets as collateral.

Since much of that collateral is worth far less than its value on paper, the Fed will be on the hook for huge potential losses. Thus, some analysts call the TALF a backdoor bailout—a program that, like PPIP, is designed primarily to off-load toxic assets onto the federal government.

The *Financial Times* predicts that once the TALF is fully implemented, the Fed's balance sheet will approach $4 trillion, nearly a third of the size of the U.S. economy. That's uncharted territory.

Won't all this lead to inflation?

That's certainly possible. But the Fed and the Obama administration are far more worried about deflation—a vicious downward spiral in prices that can set in as an economy shrinks.

Widespread falling prices suppress economic growth—why buy now if prices will be lower later on? Deflation also makes debt burdens even greater. That's because the dollar amount of the debt becomes ever higher in relation to the prices of commodities—which is exactly what happened during the Great Depression.

There's another important dimension to the U.S. efforts to expand the money supply—namely, a drop in value of the dollar in relation to other major currencies, like the euro and the yen. Imports to the United States therefore become more expensive, while American exports are cheaper. The economic textbooks call this a "competitive currency devaluation," a tactic that's historically been used by one country to foist the cost of the crisis onto others.

Also, a devalued dollar has the effect of effectively reducing U.S. debts to China, where banks hold upward of $1 trillion of U.S. government and government-backed bonds. The Chinese government has complained about this, and even raised the idea of creating a new international currency to replace the dollar. But for now, China is stuck with U.S. dollars, which remain the safest form of investment, if only because the alternatives are so much worse.

Will the agreements at the Group of 20 (G-20) [a group of the world's most industrialized nations] summit in London [in April 2009] spur an economic recovery internationally?

The slumping world economy has put the leaders of the G-20 countries under growing political pressure.

The IMF predicts that the global economy will shrink this year [2009] by between 0.5 and 1 percent, while the World Bank anticipates a contraction of 1.7 percent. The Organisation for Economic Co-operation and Development, the group of leading industrialized countries, predicts the world economy will contract by 2.75 percent.

But rather than drive world leaders toward international cooperation, the crisis has instead brought rivalries into the open. Most notably, the United States failed to convince Germany and other major European countries to boost their economies by running up government budget deficits.

What international capitalism needs to revive, therefore, is a major reordering of the world economy.

Essentially, Germany refuses to allow its economy to bear the cost of bailing out the European Union's weakest economies in Eastern Europe. For its part, the United States staved off attempts to create a new system of international financial regulation.

The world's richest countries did agree to boost funding for the IMF to $1 trillion. That money will be used to finance emergency loans to the so-called "emerging economies" in Eastern Europe, Asia, Africa and Latin America. But the IMF will, as usual, use these funds to give the major economic powers leverage over the smaller and weaker countries.

Even if the United States does experience an economic revival by the end of 2009 or early 2010—and that's a big "if"—long-term problems remain for the world economy.

That's because the United States can no longer use consumer debt to become the world's importer of last resort. This means China, in particular, must transform an economy that's overwhelmingly geared to exports into one with a bigger internal consumer market—a complex, and perhaps impossible, transition.

What international capitalism needs to revive, therefore, is a major reordering of the world economy. That's a process that will take many years—and if capital has its way, the tremendous costs involved will be borne by workers.

The story doesn't end there, however. In a growing number of countries—most dramatically in Greece and France—workers are taking to the streets with widespread strikes and protest. Such resistance is needed in the United States as well—both to challenge the bailout to the banks and to force workers' needs into the political agenda.

CHAPTER 3

Is the Growing U.S. Debt a Threat to Americans?

Chapter Preface

The economic stimulus actions taken by former president George W. Bush and President Obama, along with the costs of the Iraq and Afghanistan wars, are expected to balloon the U.S. national debt to historic proportions. An April 2009 report from the Congressional Budget Office (CBO), a federal agency that provides economic research to Congress, found that the budget deficit has already hit $1 trillion, $640 billion more than the same time in 2008, when the deficit was a mere $313 billion. The CBO said that the sharp increase is attributable to the massive stimulus spending as well as government receipts that were $160 billion lower than those in 2008, largely because of the recession. The U.S. government borrows money by issuing Treasury bonds that offer interest to buyers, and the buyers include not only individuals, but also foreign countries. In fact, most of America's national debt is held by foreign creditors, and the largest foreign creditor is China, which now owns almost ten percent of U.S. public debt.

China officially became the largest U.S. creditor as of September 2008, when it surpassed Japan for this title. This status means that the United States is relying on China, along with other countries, to finance the U.S. economic bailout, giving foreign nations increasing influence over the American economy. In fact, some policy makers fear that China's creditor status gives it too much political leverage over the United States since it could cease buying U.S. bonds or sell its U.S. investments—an action that could devalue the U.S. currency (the dollar), make imports more costly for Americans, and raise interest rates for mortgages and other consumer loans within the United States. A decision by China to move out of U.S. government bonds could also force the United States to pay higher interest on its Treasury bonds sold abroad, driving up the cost of U.S. borrowing and making it difficult for the United States to fund stimulus, military, or social programs critical to future U.S. economic prospects. Fears about China were heightened in 2009 when Chinese officials expressed concerns about the safety of its U.S. investments, asking the Obama administration to guarantee bonds held by China. According to some reports, China has already begun to slow down its purchases of U.S. mortgage bonds, an action that pressured the U.S. government to raise mortgage rates just as it needed to lower them to deal with the sinking U.S. economy.

On the other hand, if China continues to invest in U.S. debt, economic experts say that too could produce negative economic consequences for the United States. Such foreign investments make the U.S. dollar stronger against the Chinese currency (the yuan), causing U.S. exports to be more expensive, and making it harder for U.S. companies to sell their products overseas. This situation has actually been the status quo for many years and has created a large trade deficit between the two countries. In fact, many U.S. commentators charge that China has bought U.S. debt to deliberately keep the Chinese yuan artificially weak to boost Chinese exports and fuel its rapid economic rise. In one sense, this balance has also been good for America; throughout recent decades, many of these Chinese goods have been purchased by American consumers, giving them access to cheap televisions and other goods. Yet the weak yuan/strong dollar scenario has also been blamed by many commentators for creating and helping to sustain the low U.S. interest rates that encouraged the housing bubble, which in turn sparked the current U.S. and worldwide recession.

For these and other reasons, many economists see the growing economic interdependence between China and the United States as unhealthy for the long term. Ideally, the two countries during the next decade will find ways to work together to lower the trade deficit and reduce overall U.S. debt, to bring more balance to their economic relationship. In fact, some commentators suggest that the current recession and rising U.S. deficit, if it causes China to back away from buying U.S. debt, could help to create this better balance. If the value of the dollar lowers and the value of the Chinese yuan increases, U.S. manufacturers will stand a better chance of breaking into the vast Chinese consumer markets—a healthy adjustment that U.S. policy makers have been pursuing for many years.

The relationship with China and its effect on the United States' economic future is only one of the concerns surrounding the growing U.S. debt. Whether this debt, and the nation's deficit spending to recover from the 2007–2009 recession, is a true threat to the United States is the subject of the viewpoints in this chapter.

President Obama's Deficit Spending Could Trigger a Future Financial Crisis

Robert J. Samuelson

Robert J. Samuelson is a weekly columnist for the Washington Post, *a daily American newspaper published in Washington, D.C.*

Just how much government debt does a president have to endorse before he's labeled "irresponsible"? Well, apparently much more than the massive amounts envisioned by President [Barack] Obama. The final version of his 2010 budget, released last week [May 2009], is a case study in political expediency and economic gambling.

Astonishing Debt Numbers

Let's see. From 2010 to 2019, Obama projects annual deficits totaling $7.1 trillion; that's atop the $1.8 trillion deficit for 2009. By 2019, the ratio of publicly held federal debt to gross domestic product (GDP, or the economy) would reach 70 percent, up from 41 percent in 2008. That would be the highest since 1950 (80 percent). The Congressional Budget Office [also known as CBO, a federal agency that provides economic research for Congress], using less optimistic economic forecasts, raises these estimates. The 2010–19 deficits would total $9.3 trillion; the debt-to-GDP ratio in 2019 would be 82 percent.

But wait: Even these totals may be understated. By various estimates, Obama's health plan might cost $1.2 trillion over a decade; Obama has budgeted only $635 billion. Next, the huge deficits occur despite a pronounced squeeze of defense spend-

Robert J. Samuelson, "Obama's Risky Debt," *Washington Post*, May 18, 2009. Reprinted with permission.

ing. From 2008 to 2019, total federal spending would rise 75 percent, but defense spending would increase only 17 percent. Unless foreign threats recede, military spending and deficits might both grow.

Except from crabby Republicans, these astonishing numbers have received little attention—a tribute to Obama's Zen-like capacity to discourage serious criticism. Everyone's fixated on the present economic crisis, which explains and justifies big deficits (lost revenue, anti-recession spending) for a few years. Hardly anyone notes that huge deficits continue indefinitely.

One reason Obama is so popular is that he has promised almost everyone lower taxes and higher spending. Beyond the undeserving who make more than $250,000, 95 percent of "working families" receive a tax cut. Obama would double federal spending for basic research in "key agencies." He wants to build high-speed-rail networks that would require continuous subsidy. Obama can do all this and more by borrowing.

Consider the extra debt as a proxy for political evasion. The president doesn't want to confront Americans with choices between lower spending and higher taxes—or, given the existing deficits, perhaps both *less spending and more taxes*. Except for talk, Obama hasn't done anything to reduce the expense of retiring baby boomers. He claims to be containing overall health costs, but he's actually proposing more government spending.

At worst, the burgeoning debt could trigger a future financial crisis.

Cutting the Deficit

Closing future deficits with either tax increases or spending cuts would require gigantic changes. Discounting the recession's effect on the deficit, Marc Goldwein of the Committee for a Responsible Federal Budget puts the underlying "structural deficit"—the basic gap between the government's spending commitments and its tax base—at 3 to 4 percent of GDP. In today's dollars, that's roughly $400 billion to $600 billion.

It's true that since 1961 the federal budget has run deficits in all but five years. But the resulting government debt has consistently remained below 50 percent of GDP; that's the equivalent of a household with $100,000 of income having a $50,000 debt. (Note: Deficits are the annual gap between government's spending and its tax revenue. The debt is the total borrowing caused by past deficits.) Adverse economic effects, if any, were modest. But Obama's massive, future deficits would break this pattern and become more threatening.

At best, the rising cost of the debt would intensify pressures to increase taxes, cut spending—or create bigger, unsustainable deficits. By the CBO's estimates, interest on the debt as a share of federal spending will double between 2008 and 2019, to 16 percent. Huge budget deficits could also weaken economic growth by "crowding out" private investment.

At worst, the burgeoning debt could trigger a future financial crisis. The danger is that "we won't be able to sell [Treasury debt] at reasonable interest rates," says economist Rudy Penner, head of the CBO from 1983 to 1987. In today's anxious climate, this hasn't happened. American and foreign investors have favored "safe" U.S. Treasurys. But a glut of bonds, fears of inflation—or something else—might one day shatter confidence. Bond prices might fall sharply; interest rates would rise. The consequences could be worldwide because foreigners own half of U.S. Treasury debt.

The Obama budgets flirt with deferred distress, though we can't know what form it might take or when it might occur. Present gain comes with the risk of future pain. As the present economic crisis shows, imprudent policies ultimately backfire, even if the reversal's timing and nature are unpredictable.

The wonder is that these issues have been so ignored. Imagine hypothetically that a President [John] McCain had submitted a budget plan identical to Obama's. There would almost certainly have been a loud outcry: "McCain's Mortgaging Our Future." Obama should be held to no less exacting a standard.

Foreign Creditors Will Not Buy Unlimited Amounts of U.S. Debt

Peter Schiff

Peter Schiff is the president of Euro Pacific Capital, an investment company, and is the author of The Little Book of Bull Moves in Bear Markets.

Barack Obama has spoken often of sacrifice. And as recently as a week ago [January 2009], he said that to stave off the deepening recession Americans should be prepared to face "trillion dollar deficits for years to come."

But apart from a stirring call for volunteerism in his inaugural address, the only specific sacrifices the president has outlined thus far include lower taxes, millions of federally funded jobs, expanded corporate bailouts, and direct stimulus checks to consumers. Could this be described as sacrificial?

It seems inconceivable to President Obama, or any respected economist for that matter, that our creditors may decline to sign on.

Relying on Creditor Nations

What he might have said was that the nations funding the majority of America's public debt—most notably the Chinese, Japanese and the Saudis—need to be prepared to sacrifice. They have to fund America's annual trillion-dollar deficits for the foreseeable future. These creditor nations, who already own trillions of dollars of U.S. government debt, are the only entities capable of underwriting the spending that Mr. Obama envisions and that U.S. citizens demand.

Peter Schiff, "The World Won't Buy Unlimited U.S. Debt: We're Asking Others to Sacrifice for Our 'Stimulus,'" *Wall Street Journal*, January 23, 2009. Reproduced by permission of the author.

These nations, in other words, must never use the money to buy other assets or fund domestic spending initiatives for their own people. When the old Treasury bills mature, they can do nothing with the money except buy new ones. To do otherwise would implode the market for U.S. Treasurys (sending U.S. interest rates much higher) and start a run on the dollar.

In sum, our creditors must give up all hope of accessing the principal, and may be compensated only by the paltry 2%–3% yield our bonds currently deliver.

As absurd as this may appear on the surface, it seems inconceivable to President Obama, or any respected economist for that matter, that our creditors may decline to sign on. Their confidence is derived from the fact that the arrangement has gone on for some time, and that our creditors would be unwilling to face the economic turbulence that would result from an interruption of the status quo.

But just because the game has lasted thus far does not mean that they will continue playing it indefinitely. Thanks to projected huge deficits, the U.S. government is severely raising the stakes. At the same time, the global economic contraction will make larger Treasury purchases by foreign central banks both economically and politically more difficult.

Economic Contraction and Higher Debt

The root problem is not that America may have difficulty borrowing enough from abroad to maintain our GDP [gross domestic product, a measure of a country's total economic output], but that our economy was too large in the first place. America's GDP is composed of more than 70% consumer spending. For many years, much of that spending has been a function of voracious consumer borrowing through home equity extractions (averaging more than $850 billion annually in 2005 and 2006, according to the Federal Reserve) and rapid expansion of credit card and other consumer debt. Now that credit is scarce, it is inevitable that GDP will fall.

Neither the left nor the right of the American political spectrum has shown any willingness to tolerate such a contraction. Recently, for example, Nobel Prize–winning economist Paul Krugman estimated that a 6.8% contraction in GDP will result in $2.1 trillion in "lost output," which the government should redeem through fiscal stimulation. In his view, the $775 billion announced in Mr. Obama's plan is two-thirds too small.

If any other country were to face these conditions, unpalatable measures such as severe government austerity or currency devaluation would be the only options.

Although Mr. Krugman may not get all that he wishes, it is clear that Mr. Obama's opening bid will likely move north considerably before any legislation is passed. It is also clear from the political chatter that the policies most favored will be those that encourage rapid consumer spending, not lasting or sustainable economic change. So when the effects of this stimulus dissipate, the same unbalanced economy will remain—only now with a far higher debt load.

If any other country were to face these conditions, unpalatable measures such as severe government austerity or currency devaluation would be the only options. But with our currency's reserve status, we have much more attractive alternatives. We are planning to spend as much as we like, for as long as we like, and we will let the rest of the world pick up the tab.

Currently, U.S. citizens comprise less than 5% of world population, but account for more than 25% of global GDP. Given our debts and weakening economy, this disproportionate advantage should narrow. Yet the United States is asking much poorer foreign nations to maintain the status quo, and incredibly, they are complying. At least for now.

You can't blame the Obama administration for choosing to go down this path. If these other nations are giving, it becomes very easy to take. However, given his supposedly post-ideological pragmatic gifts, one would hope that Mr. Obama can see that, just like all other bubbles in world history, the U.S. debt bubble will end badly. Taking on more debt to maintain spending is neither sacrificial nor beneficial.

President Obama Is Serious About Cutting Deficit Spending Once the Economic Crisis Is Resolved

Associated Press

Associated Press is a global news network that provides news and other information to various newspapers and media outlets.

As the federal budget deficit soars into the stratosphere, Treasury Secretary Timothy Geithner is reassuring the Chinese—the largest holders of U.S. government debt—that the Obama administration is serious about restoring fiscal discipline once the current economic crisis is resolved.

The U.S. Message to the Chinese

Geithner, making his first trip to China as Treasury secretary, used a major economic policy address Monday [June 1, 2009] as well as separate meetings with top Chinese officials to deliver that message.

"As we recover from this unprecedented crisis, we will cut our fiscal deficit, we will eliminate the extraordinary government support that we have put in place to overcome the crisis," Geithner said in a speech to students at Peking University, which Geithner attended as a young college student learning Chinese nearly three decades ago.

A Skeptical Response

The Chinese officials did not comment publicly on Geithner's reassurances, but judging from the reaction of the college students, Geithner may still have some explaining to do.

Associated Press, "Geithner Says US Concerned About the Deficits," *Dayton Daily News*, June 1, 2009. Reprinted with permission of the Associated Press.

The students peppered the Treasury secretary with questions about the debt, the administration's massive amounts of support to the banks and U.S. auto companies and the recent rise in interest rates on Treasury securities.

The recent rise in long-term rates for Treasury securities was . . . a reflection of the view by investors that the global economy is improving.

Some students wanted to know whether China's holdings of $768 billion of U.S. Treasury securities—which makes China America's biggest creditor—were safe, given projections by the Obama administration that the deficit for this year will soar to an astronomical $1.84 trillion, four times the previous single-year record.

Some students wondered whether the recent rise in interest rates was a signal that investors are beginning to worry that U.S. budget deficits will threaten inflation, weaken the dollar and reduce the value of the Chinese holdings.

China's investments in the United States "are very safe," Geithner told the students. "We have the deepest, most liquid financial markets in the world."

He said the recent rise in long-term rates for Treasury securities was not a reflection of worries about rising U.S. budget deficits but a reflection of the view by investors that the global economy is improving, which lessens demand for U.S. Treasuries as a safe haven.

As far as spending large amounts of money to support Chrysler and General Motors as they go through bankruptcy filings, Geithner said the administration was optimistic that government support would only be temporary. "We want to have a quick, clean exit," he said.

General Motors filed for Chapter 11 bankruptcy on Monday as part of an administration plan to shrink the automaker to a sustainable size with support from an additional $30 billion from the government's bailout fund.

Geithner also stressed to the students that the administration would soon unveil a comprehensive overhaul of financial system regulations designed to fix the flaws exposed by the current crisis, the worst to hit the U.S. economy since the Great Depression.

China's huge holdings of Treasury debt represent the billions of dollars that have been transferred over the years into Chinese hands to pay for America's soaring trade deficits.

He said the changes would make federal regulations "smarter and more effective" by strengthening oversight of hedge funds and derivatives, consolidating and streamlining banking regulation and providing the government with the necessary tools to shut down large financial institutions that are posing a risk to the entire system.

"We have a lot to do, but we are going to fix this," he pledged.

Efforts to Improve Relations with China

Later, Geithner and other Treasury officials met at the Great Hall of the People with a team of economic officials from China led by Vice Premier Wang Qishan for discussions about the upcoming high-level talks in Washington this summer between the two nations.

At the start of the session, Geithner said, "The world has a huge stake in our two countries working closely together to lay a foundation for recovery."

Wang called the upcoming talks, which will replace the Strategic Economic Dialogue begun in the [George W.] Bush administration, an "important initiative in growing the China-U.S. relationship."

Geithner will wrap up his visit Tuesday with meetings with Chinese President Hu Jintao and Premier Wen Jiabao. Wen sent shockwaves through global financial markets in March when he publicly expressed worries about the soaring U.S. budget deficits and what that meant "about the safety of our assets."

China's huge holdings of Treasury debt represent the billions of dollars that have been transferred over the years into Chinese hands to pay for America's soaring trade deficits.

Previous Treasury secretaries have lectured the Chinese about the need to allow their currency, the yuan, to rise in value against the dollar as a way of lowering those trade deficits by making Chinese goods more expensive and thus less desirable for American consumers and U.S. products cheaper in China.

But Geithner did not issue the same demands, part of a campaign by the Obama administration to pursue improved relations with China in hopes of getting a better outcome on economic tensions and in other areas. The administration needs support from China on a host of foreign policy issues, including North Korea's recent testing of nuclear weapons.

Geithner praised the role China is playing in stimulating the global economy. It has unveiled a sizable economic stimulus program, second only to the U.S. program.

He said that a successful transition to a more balanced and stable global economy will require substantial changes to economic policy and financial regulation around the world and especially in the United States and China, the world's largest and third largest economies.

Geithner said he believed the first steps toward a global recovery were occurring, which raised hopes the world "will succeed in averting financial collapse and global deflation."

Deficit Spending to Prevent Economic, Environmental, or Social Disasters Is Justified

Joe Conason

Joe Conason is a journalist, an author, and a political commentator who writes a column for the weekly New York Observer *newspaper and for Salon.com, a news Web site.*

[Former vice president] Dick Cheney once observed that "deficits don't matter," which may well have been the most honest phrase he ever uttered. His words were at least partly true, which is more than can be said for the great majority of the vice president's remarks—and they certainly expressed the candid attitude of Republicans whenever they attain power. His pithy fiscal slogan should remind us that much of the current political furor over deficit spending in the [President Barack] Obama budget is wrong, hypocritical, and worthy of the deepest skepticism.

A History of Deficits

In our time, the Republican Party has compiled an impressive history of talking about fiscal responsibility while running up unrivaled deficits and debt. Of the roughly $11 trillion in federal debt accumulated to date, more than 90 percent can be attributed to the tenure of three presidents: Ronald Reagan, who used to complain constantly about runaway spending; George Herbert Walker Bush, reputed to be one of those old-fashioned green-eyeshade Republicans; and his spendthrift son George "Dubya" Bush, whose trillion-dollar war and irrespon-

Joe Conason, "Dick Cheney Was Right: Deficits Don't Matter—and Republicans Who Are Complaining About Barack Obama's Spending Are Hypocrites," Salon.com, March 27, 2009. www.salon.com. This article first appeared in Salon.com, at http://www.salon.com. An online version remains in the Salon archives. Reprinted with permission.

sible tax cuts accounted for nearly half the entire burden. Only [former president] Bill Clinton temporarily reversed the trend with surpluses and started to pay down the debt (by raising rates on the wealthiest taxpayers).

Republicans in Congress likewise demanded balanced budgets in their propaganda (as featured in the 1993 Contract with America), but then proceeded to despoil the Treasury with useless spending and tax cuts for those who needed them least. Even [Senator] John McCain, once a principled critic of those tax cuts, turned hypocrite when he endorsed them while continuing to denounce the deficits they had caused.

But was Cheney wrong when he airily dismissed the importance of deficits? In the full quotation, as first recounted by Paul O'Neill, Bush's fired Treasury secretary, he said, "You know, Paul, Reagan proved deficits don't matter. We won the [congressional] midterms [in November 2002]. This is our due." What he evidently meant—aside from claiming the spoils—was that the effects of deficit spending tend to be less dire than predicted. And that insight deserves to be considered if only because all the partisan barking over the projected deficits in the Obama budget is so hysterical—as if nothing could be worse than more federal spending.

Such is the institutional bias of the Washington press corps, which habitually refers to deficits "exploding" and to the nation "engulfed in red ink," and so on. But in fact the United States has recovered from considerably deeper indebtedness than that now on the horizon. Besides, as history warns, there are things much worse than deficits and debt. One such thing was the Great Depression, prolonged when [President] Franklin Roosevelt decided to curb the deficits that had revived the economy, and ended only when he raised spending even higher in wartime. Another was worldwide fascist domination, a threat defeated by expanding America's public debt to unprecedented levels during World War II. No sane person cared then that public debt had risen well above gross domestic product.

Those scary charts and graphs often deployed to illustrate our parlous state of indebtedness rarely date back as far as the forties and fifties—and the reason is simple. The massive deficits incurred during the war didn't matter, as Cheney might say, because the wartime national investments in industry, technology and science undergirded a postwar boom that lasted for nearly three decades, creating the largest and most prosperous middle class in human history.

President Obama is more troubled by the enormous threats to the nation's future than by deficits, even if they are projected in trillions of dollars.

The average annual growth rate remained close to four percent for that entire period—and over time the combination of constant growth and smaller deficits reduced the ratio of debt to a fraction of its postwar dimension. What mattered more than the size of the deficits was whether they were spent on things that enabled consistent growth.

Deficit Spending Is Justified

Today, President Obama is more troubled by the enormous threats to the nation's future than by deficits, even if they are projected in trillions of dollars. Clearly he believes that there are still some things worse than debt.

One such thing would be a global depression that drags on for several years. Another would be the catastrophic consequences of unchecked climate change, potentially more devastating than a world war; deteriorating public schools that will undermine democracy and demote us to secondary status; and a national health system that costs too much, provides too little care, and burdens enterprise. By investing now, he hopes to prevent disaster and create the conditions for sustainable expansion.

Not all of the warnings about deficit spending are false. Wasteful federal spending can eventually lead to inflation; excessive deficits can cause interest rates to rise, although that doesn't always occur. But as Clinton proved in confronting the huge legacy of debt left over from the Reagan era, it is possible to raise taxes and slow spending without damage to the broader economy.

As for the Republicans, it is difficult to listen to their doomsaying predictions without laughing. They want us to worry about the evils of deficit spending when they obviously don't worry about that at all. Just yesterday [March 26, 2009], the House Republican leadership distributed what they called an alternative budget. Missing from that thin sheaf of papers was any attempt to estimate what their plan would cost and how much it would increase the deficit. Their ironic ignorance of history was illustrated by their single concrete proposal. They insist that we must cut the maximum tax rate from 36 percent to 25 percent—or the same as the top rate in 1929, on the eve of the Great Depression.

There Are No Dire Consequences if China Stops Buying U.S. Debt

Dean Baker

Dean Baker is cofounder and codirector of the Center for Economic and Policy Research, a Washington-based think tank focusing on economic policy.

When China's prime minister, Wen Jiabao, expressed concern about the ability of the US government to repay its bonds, his comments prompted headlines everywhere. The newspapers were filled with gloomy warnings that China may no longer be willing to buy up US debt, which supposedly would have dire consequences for us all.

No Dire Consequences

Unfortunately, too little thought was given to what these "dire consequences" might be, and who would end up suffering them. Suppose that China stops buying US government debt. That would mean that the dollar would plummet in value against the yuan [China's currency]. Chinese imports would suddenly become much more expensive for consumers in the United States, making domestically produced items far more competitive.

The opposite would happen in China. Goods and services made in the United States would suddenly be much cheaper. As a result, we would expect to export much more to China, and see many more Chinese come to the United States as tourists or for business purposes. The reduction in imports from China and the increase in exports would substantially improve our balance of trade.

Dean Baker, "China's Empty Threat: If Wen Jiabao Stops Buying US Debt, China's Currency Will Rise—Which Is What America Has Wanted All Along," *Guardian*, March 30, 2009. www.guardian.co.uk. Reproduced by permission of Guardian News Service, LTD.

In other words, if Wen was threatening to stop buying dollar-denominated assets and therefore let the yuan rise against the dollar, he was threatening to do exactly what the US government has been demanding that China do. He will stop "manipulating" China's currency—meaning he will stop deliberately intervening in the market to keep the yuan's value from rising.

There is an alternative interpretation of Wen's threat. Perhaps he will stop buying long-term government bonds, but continue to buy short-term debt. This will have some impact on raising long-term interest rates in the United States, but it hardly provides a basis for panic.

The reason that Wen's threat should not be serious cause for concern is that if we want to keep long-term interest rates low, we already have a mechanism: It's called the Federal Reserve Board [the Fed, the nation's central bank, which controls monetary policy]. Just last week Federal Reserve Chairman Ben Bernanke announced that he was going to buy up more than $1tn [trillion] in long-term government or agency (Fannie Mae and Freddie Mac) bonds over the next several months. This purchase far exceeds any possible purchases of long bonds by the Chinese. If Wen pulls out of the market, Bernanke can simply increase his purchases to offset the lost demand.

Does this policy risk inflation? Actually, the Chinese purchase of Treasury bills and the Fed's buying up the long-term bonds would have the same impact on inflation. It really doesn't matter whether the Chinese government or the Fed is buying bonds to hold down the long-term interest rate—the impact on the inflation rate will be the same. Of course in a period where there are serious concerns about deflation, a modest increase in the inflation rate would be a good thing.

China's Policy of Currency Manipulation

There is one other irony about Wen's threat that is worth noting. In 2004, [former Federal Reserve chairman] Alan Greenspan began to raise short-term interest rates. He expressed surprise that long-term interest rates stayed constant or even fell slightly. He described this as a "conundrum".

There was actually nothing mysterious about the situation at all. As Greenspan was acting to raise short-term interest rates, the Chinese and other foreign central banks were intervening directly in the long-term market, buying up long-term bonds in order to keep long-term interests down. Did Greenspan fail to recognise the impact of the Chinese intervention in the same way that he managed to miss an $8tn [trillion] housing bubble?

We always knew that China would not subsidise its exports to the United States forever.

In short, Wen has nothing with which to threaten the United States. He is proposing to do something that Congress and the [George W.] Bush and [Barack] Obama administrations have all urged him to do: stop propping up the value of the dollar against the yuan.

This will lead to an adjustment process involving some pain on both sides. In China's case, the reduction in exports to the United States will require increasing the size of its domestic market, or at least finding alternative destinations for its exports. In the case of the United States, we will have to pay more for our imports, which will mean some increase in the rate of inflation and, in the short term, a modest decline in our standard of living.

But we always knew that China would not subsidise its exports to the United States forever. It would have been better for us if they had stopped a decade ago, before we developed a huge trade imbalance and developed a housing bubble–led growth path. Still, better late than never. Wen has made a promise, not a threat—and we should encourage him to follow through on it.

Chapter 4

How Can the Government Stabilize the U.S. Economy in the Future?

Chapter Preface

As the recession in the U.S. economy unfolded in the fall of 2007 and throughout 2008 and 2009, many of the nation's largest banks came close to insolvency as the downturn in the housing market spread to the banking sector. As a result, banks across the country virtually stopped lending to conserve their capital, and consumers were prevented from getting loans to buy homes, cars, or other items, making the recession even worse. Some of the biggest U.S. banks, including Citibank, Bank of America, HSBC Bank USA, Wells Fargo, and JPMorgan Chase, faced potentially huge losses from derivatives—a type of complicated financial product dependent on the value of a secondary asset. Many of these bank-owned derivatives were mortgage-backed securities—basically bundles of home mortgage loans with values that were plummeting due to dropping housing prices and borrowers who had taken on risky loans.

To rescue the failing banks and help slow the recession, the government in late 2008 felt compelled to authorize $700 billion in federal funding for a massive bailout program called the Troubled Asset Relief Program (TARP). In addition to this government bailout, many policy makers and commentators seemed to agree that, as part of the economic recovery, the government needed to better regulate the nation's banking activities to avoid a similar economic crisis in the future. Much of the attention in the press focused on the United States' existing regulatory system for banks and how it failed to prevent the recession.

Understanding the current state of bank regulation, however, requires a review of the Glass-Steagall Act (GSA), a law enacted in the wake of the Great Depression that was subsequently repealed. The GSA, officially named the Banking Act of 1933, was passed by the Congress on June 16, 1933, following the collapse of a large portion of the American commercial banking system. The 1933 act separated banks into two types—commercial and investment banks; in addition, it founded the Federal Deposit Insurance Corporation (FDIC) to federally insure bank deposits. A number of commentators have noted that the 1933 banking failure was similar to today's banking crisis because it was caused by banks taking on too many risky investments. In the pre-Depression period, in the hope of making greater profits, banks not only unwisely invested depositors' money, but also bought investments to resell to the public. In addition, some banks adopted unethical practices, such as making loans to companies in which the bank had invested and encouraging clients to invest in those same companies. The GSA sought to stop these practices by setting up a regulatory firewall between commercial and investment bank activities and exercising more control over both sides of banking.

Under the provisions of the GSA, banks had to decide whether they would specialize in commercial or in investment banking. In addition, to prevent a situation in which banks might use deposits to cover their investment losses, the GSA required that only 10 percent of commercial banks' total income could stem from securities. A later piece of legislation, the Bank Holding Company Act of 1957, placed further limitations on banks by preventing them from underwriting insurance, a practice also considered too risky for the banking industry.

In the decades that followed, the GSA regulatory system was considered by some observers to be highly successful, since it prevented another Great Depression–type banking crisis. Many economists, however, argued that the system was too restrictive and that it actually made the banking industry more risky because banks could no longer diversify their investments to reduce risk. These critics also said that modern banks must be much more transparent about their financial holdings, lessening the risk that they would make bad investments. These arguments ultimately won over the Congress in 1999, when it passed by an overwhelming majority the Financial Services Modernization Act (also known as the Gramm-Leach-Bliley Act)—legislation that repealed the GSA. Under the new law, the barrier between commercial and investment banks was eliminated and banks were once again permitted to offer investment services and underwrite insurance. Banks could now sell insurance and stocks, and were no longer burdened by heavy regulations.

The current recession has sparked calls for new bank regulations similar to those put in place by the GSA. Many commentators argue that the repeal of GSA led directly to the modern banking crisis because it allowed the country's largest banks to once again take on too many risky investments without proper government oversight. Banks also were allowed to grow in size, becoming too big to fail—that is, too important to the U.S. economy to be allowed to go bankrupt, forcing the government bailouts. The debate about bank regulation, however, is but one of the issues confronting the U.S. government as it grapples with how to help the economy recover from the current recession. The authors of the viewpoints in this chapter present a number of ideas for how to stabilize the U.S. economy in the future.

More Fiscal Stimulus Is Needed to Reverse the Economic Decline

Mark Weisbrot

Mark Weisbrot is codirector of the Center for Economic and Policy Research, a public policy think tank located in Washington, D.C.

In February [2009] the Congress approved $787 billion of federal spending, in order keep the economy from sinking into a deeper recession. However, it is increasingly clear that this is not enough, and a third stimulus (the first was a small stimulus package early last year) will be necessary.

A Shrinking Economy

About $584 billion of the stimulus package will be spent over the next two years, in order [to] keep the economy from sinking into a deeper recession. This sounds like a lot of money, but it is only about two percent of gross domestic product (GDP) [a measure of a country's economic output] over the next two years. Our economy shrank at an annual rate of 6.3 percent in the fourth quarter of last year [2008]; economists surveyed by the *Wall Street Journal* project negative 1.4 percent for 2009, with recovery beginning in the second half. However, these forecasts have been overoptimistic in the past—most economists missed the housing bubble and the disastrous impacts of its inevitable collapse.

In short, we really don't know where the bottom of the recession is, or whether a prolonged period of high unemployment and weak growth will follow. There has been a lot of

Mark Weisbrot, "More Fiscal Stimulus Is Needed to Reverse Economic Decline," Center for Economic and Policy Research, April 14, 2009. www.cepr.net. Reproduced by permission.

emphasis on curing the ills of the financial system, and this is surely necessary for a sustained recovery to take hold. However, it is not sufficient. Even if the U.S. Treasury's latest plan were to restore solvency to the entire financial system—and this seems very unlikely—we would still be facing a serious recession in the real economy. Even solvent banks are not going to increase lending if there are no additional credit-worthy borrowers seeking loans.

The Data

The latest data on home prices reinforce this point. The decline in home prices is still accelerating, with the 20-city [S&P/]Case-Shiller index [a gauge of U.S. home prices] falling at an annual rate of 26.5 percent over the last quarter. Home prices have further to fall to get back to their pre-bubble trend levels, and they could even overshoot on the downside: People who lose equity in their homes when prices fall cannot afford a down payment (now raised to 20 percent) for a new home when they have to move, and rising unemployment and foreclosures add to the oversupply of housing.

The global economic outlook is also worsening, with the OECD [Organisation for Economic Co-operation and Development, an organization that helps governments develop their economies] now forecasting a phenomenal 2.75 GDP percent decline worldwide. Although the United States is fortunate in this respect to export only about 11 percent of GDP, shrinking global demand and an overvalued dollar do not offer much hope for trade to boost the U.S. recovery.

The household savings rate collapsed to zero in 2007, from an average of 8 percent in the post–World War II era. As savings recover to more normal levels, it means that consumption, which is about 70 percent of the economy, must fall. This can also further discourage investment and add to the cycle of declining output and employment, as well as the fear and pessimism that exacerbates it.

My colleague Dean Baker has put forth a plan for the government to provide a tax credit to employers for health care and also to increase employees' paid time off—in the form of reduced hours, additional vacation, sick leave, or other days off. This has the advantage of injecting money very quickly into the economy with minimal bureaucracy or waste. If these credits cause employers to reduce average hours per worker by just three percent, this would add 4.2 million jobs at the same level of output.

With the collapse of private spending, it is clearly up to the government to rescue the real economy, and ideological prejudices must be swept aside. It is time for our government to consider some fresh ideas that can be implemented quickly.

The United States Must Break Up the Big Banks' Financial Oligarchy to Achieve True Reform

Simon Johnson

Simon Johnson is a professor at MIT's Sloan School of Management, and he was the chief economist at the International Monetary Fund during 2007 and 2008.

In its depth and suddenness, the U.S. economic and financial crisis is shockingly reminiscent of moments we have recently seen in emerging markets (and only in emerging markets): South Korea (1997), Malaysia (1998), Russia and Argentina (time and again). In each of those cases, global investors, afraid that the country or its financial sector wouldn't be able to pay off mountainous debt, suddenly stopped lending. And in each case, that fear became self-fulfilling, as banks that couldn't roll over their debt did, in fact, become unable to pay. This is precisely what drove Lehman Brothers into bankruptcy on September 15 [2008], causing all sources of funding to the U.S. financial sector to dry up overnight. Just as in emerging-market crises, the weakness in the banking system has quickly rippled out into the rest of the economy, causing a severe economic contraction and hardship for millions of people.

But there's a deeper and more disturbing similarity: Elite business interests—financiers, in the case of the U.S.—played a central role in creating the crisis, making ever-larger gambles, with the implicit backing of the government, until the inevitable collapse. More alarming, they are now using their influence to prevent precisely the sorts of reforms that are needed,

Simon Johnson, "The Quiet Coup," *Atlantic*, May 2009. Reproduced by permission of the author.

and fast, to pull the economy out of its nosedive. The government seems helpless, or unwilling, to act against them.

Favored Treatment for the Financial Sector

Top investment bankers and government officials like to lay the blame for the current crisis on the lowering of U.S. interest rates after the dot-com bust or, even better—in a "buck stops somewhere else" sort of way—on the flow of savings out of China. Some on the right like to complain about Fannie Mae or Freddie Mac, or even about longer-standing efforts to promote broader homeownership. And, of course, it is axiomatic to everyone that the regulators responsible for "safety and soundness" were fast asleep at the wheel.

But these various policies—lightweight regulation, cheap money, the unwritten Chinese-American economic alliance, the promotion of home ownership—had something in common. Even though some are traditionally associated with Democrats and some with Republicans, they *all* benefited the financial sector. Policy changes that might have forestalled the crisis but would have limited the financial sector's profits . . . were ignored or swept aside.

For the past 25 years or so, finance has boomed, becoming ever more powerful.

The financial industry has not always enjoyed such favored treatment. But for the past 25 years or so, finance has boomed, becoming ever more powerful. The boom began with the [Ronald] Reagan years, and it only gained strength with the deregulatory policies of the [Bill] Clinton and George W. Bush administrations. Several other factors helped fuel the financial industry's ascent. [Former chairman of the Federal Reserve] Paul Volcker's monetary policy in the 1980s, and the increased volatility in interest rates that accompanied it, made bond trading much more lucrative. The invention of securitization, interest-rate swaps, and credit default swaps greatly increased the volume of transactions that bankers could make money on. And an aging and increasingly wealthy population invested more and more money in securities, helped by the invention of the IRA [Individual Retirement Account] and the 401(k) plan. Together, these developments vastly increased the profit opportunities in financial services.

Not surprisingly, Wall Street ran with these opportunities. From 1973 to 1985, the financial sector never earned more than 16 percent of domestic corporate profits. In 1986, that figure reached 19 percent. In the 1990s, it oscillated between 21 percent and 30 percent, higher than it had ever been in the postwar period. This decade, it reached 41 percent. Pay rose just as dramatically. From 1948 to 1982, average compensation in the financial sector ranged between 99 percent and 108 percent of the average for all domestic private industries. From 1983, it shot upward, reaching 181 percent in 2007.

Over the past decade, the attitude took hold that what was good for Wall Street was good for the country.

The great wealth that the financial sector created and concentrated gave bankers enormous political weight—a weight not seen in the U.S. since the era of [banker] J.P. Morgan. In that period, the banking panic of 1907 could be stopped only by coordination among private-sector bankers: No government entity was able to offer an effective response. But that first age of banking oligarchs came to an end with the passage of significant banking regulation in response to the Great Depression; the reemergence of an American financial oligarchy is quite recent.

The Wall Street—Washington Corridor

Of course, the U.S. is unique. And just as we have the world's most advanced economy, military, and technology, we also have its most advanced oligarchy. In a primitive political system, power is transmitted through violence, or the threat of violence: military coups, private militias, and so on. In a less primitive system more typical of emerging markets, power is transmitted via money: bribes, kickbacks, and offshore bank accounts. Although lobbying and campaign contributions certainly play major roles in the American political system, old-fashioned corruption—envelopes stuffed with $100 bills—is probably a sideshow today, Jack Abramoff [powerful lobbyist convicted of fraud and bribery] notwithstanding.

Instead, the American financial industry gained political power by amassing a kind of cultural capital—a belief system. Once, perhaps, what was good for General Motors was good for the country. Over the past decade, the attitude took hold that what was good for Wall Street was good for the country. The banking-and-securities industry has become one of the top contributors to political campaigns, but at the peak of its influence, it did not have to buy favors the way, for example, the tobacco companies or military contractors might have to. Instead, it benefited from the fact that Washington insiders already believed that large financial institutions and free-flowing capital markets were crucial to America's position in the world. . . .

From this confluence of campaign finance, personal connections, and ideology there flowed, in just the past decade, a river of deregulatory policies that is, in hindsight, astonishing:

- insistence on free movement of capital across borders;
- the repeal of Depression-era regulations separating commercial and investment banking;
- a congressional ban on the regulation of credit default swaps;
- major increases in the amount of leverage allowed to investment banks;

- a light hand at the Securities and Exchange Commission in its regulatory enforcement;

- an international agreement to allow banks to measure their own riskiness;

- and an intentional failure to update regulations so as to keep up with the tremendous pace of financial innovation.

The mood that accompanied these measures in Washington seemed to swing between nonchalance and outright celebration: Finance unleashed, it was thought, would continue to propel the economy to greater heights. . . .

The Way Out

Looking just at the financial crisis, we face at least two major, interrelated problems. The first is a desperately ill banking sector that threatens to choke off any incipient recovery that the fiscal stimulus might generate. The second is a political balance of power that gives the financial sector a veto over public policy, even as that sector loses popular support.

There is no doubt what old IMF [International Monetary Fund] hands would say: Nationalize troubled banks and break them up as necessary.

Big banks, it seems, have only gained political strength since the crisis began. And this is not surprising. With the financial system so fragile, the damage that a major bank failure could cause—Lehman was small relative to Citigroup or Bank of America—is much greater than it would be during ordinary times. The banks have been exploiting this fear as they wring favorable deals out of Washington. Bank of America obtained its second bailout package after warning the government that it might not be able to go through with the acquisition of Merrill Lynch, a prospect that Treasury did not want to consider.

The challenges the United States faces are familiar territory to the people at the IMF [International Monetary Fund, an international lending organization]. If you hid the name of the country and just showed them the numbers, there is no doubt what old IMF hands would say: Nationalize troubled banks and break them up as necessary.

In some ways, of course, the government has already taken control of the banking system. It has essentially guaranteed the liabilities of the biggest banks, and it is their only plausible source of capital today. Meanwhile, the Federal Reserve [the Fed] has taken on a major role in providing credit to the economy—the function that the private banking sector is supposed to be performing, but isn't. Yet there are limits to what the Fed can do on its own; consumers and businesses are still dependent on banks that lack the balance sheets and the incentives to make the loans the economy needs, and the government has no real control over who runs the banks, or over what they do.

To break this cycle, the government must force the banks to acknowledge the scale of their problems. . . . [T]he most direct way to do this is nationalization.

At the root of the banks' problems are the large losses they have undoubtedly taken on their securities and loan portfolios. But they don't want to recognize the full extent of their losses, because that would likely expose them as insolvent. So they talk down the problem, and ask for handouts that aren't enough to make them healthy, but are enough to keep them upright a little longer. This behavior is corrosive: Unhealthy banks either don't lend (hoarding money to shore up reserves) or they make desperate gambles on high-risk loans and investments that could pay off big, but probably won't pay off at all. In either case, the economy suffers further, and as it does, bank assets themselves continue to deteriorate—creating a highly destructive vicious cycle.

To break this cycle, the government must force the banks to acknowledge the scale of their problems. As the IMF understands (and as the U.S. government itself has insisted to multiple emerging-market countries in the past), the most direct way to do this is nationalization. Instead, the Treasury is trying to negotiate bailouts bank by bank, and behaving as if the banks hold all the cards—contorting the terms of each deal to minimize government ownership while forswearing government influence over bank strategy or operations. Under these conditions, cleaning up bank balance sheets is impossible.

Nationalization would not imply permanent state ownership. The IMF's advice would be, essentially: scale up the standard Federal Deposit Insurance Corporation [FDIC] process. An FDIC "intervention" is basically a government-managed bankruptcy procedure for banks. It would allow the government to wipe out bank shareholders, replace failed management, clean up the balance sheets, and then sell the banks back to the private sector. The main advantage is immediate recognition of the problem so that it can be solved before it grows worse.

The government needs to inspect the balance sheets and identify the banks that cannot survive a severe recession. These banks should face a choice: write down your assets to their true value and raise private capital within 30 days, or be taken over by the government. The government would write down the toxic assets of banks taken into receivership—recognizing reality—and transfer those assets to a separate government entity, which would attempt to salvage whatever value is possible for the taxpayer (as the Resolution Trust Corporation did after the savings and loan debacle of the 1980s). The rump banks—cleansed and able to lend safely, and hence trusted again by other lenders and investors—could then be sold off.

Cleaning up the megabanks will be complex. And it will be expensive for the taxpayer; according to the latest IMF numbers, the cleanup of the banking system would probably cost close to $1.5 trillion (or 10 percent of our GDP [gross domestic product, a measure of a country's total economic output]) in the long term. But only decisive government action—exposing the full extent of the financial rot and restoring some set of banks to publicly verifiable health—can cure the financial sector as a whole.

This may seem like strong medicine. But in fact, while necessary, it is insufficient. The second problem the United States faces—the power of the oligarchy—is just as important as the immediate crisis of lending. And the advice from the IMF on this front would again be simple: Break the oligarchy.

Oversize institutions disproportionately influence public policy; the major banks we have today draw much of their power from being too big to fail. Nationalization and reprivatization would not change that; while the replacement of the bank executives who got us into this crisis would be just and sensible, ultimately, the swapping-out of one set of powerful managers for another would change only the names of the oligarchs.

Ideally, big banks should be sold in medium-size pieces, divided regionally or by type of business. Where this proves impractical—since we'll want to sell the banks quickly—they could be sold whole, but with the requirement of being broken up within a short time. Banks that remain in private hands should also be subject to size limitations.

This may seem like a crude and arbitrary step, but it is the best way to limit the power of individual institutions in a sector that is essential to the economy as a whole. Of course, some people will complain about the "efficiency costs" of a more fragmented banking system, and these costs are real. But so are the costs when a bank that is too big to fail—a financial weapon of mass self-destruction—explodes. Anything that is too big to fail is too big to exist.

To ensure systematic bank breakup, and to prevent the eventual reemergence of dangerous behemoths, we also need to overhaul our antitrust legislation. Laws put in place more than 100 years ago to combat industrial monopolies were not designed to address the problem we now face. The problem in the financial sector today is not that a given firm might have enough market share to influence prices; it is that one firm or a small set of interconnected firms, by failing, can bring down the economy. The [Barrack] Obama administration's fiscal stimulus evokes FDR [former president Franklin D. Roosevelt], but what we need to imitate here is Teddy Roosevelt's trust-busting.

The Government Should Reduce Taxes to Stimulate Economic Growth

Jimmy Sengenberger

Jimmy Sengenberger is a staff writer for Regis University High-lander, *a college newspaper in Colorado.*

The United States of America is at an impasse. Congress, pressed by President [Barack] Obama to act quickly to prevent "catastrophe," is on the verge of spending more than $800 billion on a "fiscal stimulus package" intended to jump-start the economy, with roughly $300 billion in tax rebate checks and $500 billion in infrastructure spending. [Editor's Note: The American Recovery and Reinvestment Act—President Obama's stimulus package—was signed into law on February 17, 2009.]

Hundreds of economists, however, have expressed their deep concerns about the government's plan for dealing with the recession, and a review of the effectiveness of such policies as those proposed reveals the folly of tax rebates and government spending as fiscal stimulus.

1. Tax rebates do not boost consumer spending. According to economist Martin Feldstein, CEO of the National Bureau of Economic Research [NBER], when tax rebates went out as economic stimulus last spring, only around 16% of the checks were actually spent, with nearly five times that amount going into savings. Most of the rebates were used to pay off loans, not to buy new products and services, and the stimulus package utterly failed to preclude the recession.

In 2001, tax rates were reduced and tax rebates went out to make up the difference.

Jimmy Sengenberger, "NO: Stimulate with Tax Cuts, Not Giveaways," *Regis University Highlander*, February 9, 2009. Reproduced by permission.

While the economy improved after the tax changes, evidence suggests that the rate reductions, not the rebates, did the trick. A late-2001 study conducted by economists Matthew Shapiro and Joel Slemrod of the University of Michigan and NBER found that only 22% of those households receiving stimulus checks spent the money.

Furthermore, by the time the checks would be in the mail, the economy may be improving, as happened, according to Steven Weisman and Edmund Andrews of the *New York Times*, in the 1970s. If implemented now, the benefits of a tax rebate stimulus—a small burst in increased consumer demand—are minimal at best and will not outweigh the substantial costs.

2. Faulty policy is not worth the debt risk. While the value of the dollar has lately gained in strength, it still has the potential to continue its recent decline. As its value goes down and creditors like China see their own GDPs [gross domestic product, a measure of a country's economic output] shrink, creditor concerns over their holdings of U.S. bonds will rise, resulting in the likely increase in interest as they rethink their holdings. By spending $800 billion on a stimulus package that will likely have minimal effect, the U.S. government is essentially assuming even more debt, which is already at $10.7 trillion, at greater national risk.

3. Infrastructure projects will not work. Obama intends to spend around $500 billion on infrastructure projects and public works programs, including transportation projects, intended to create jobs and boost consumer confidence. Yet when [former presidents] Herbert Hoover and FDR [Franklin D. Roosevelt] tried such programs in the 1930s to tackle the Great Depression, unemployment remained in the double digits up to World War II, averaging at 17.2%.

According to the [conservative think tank] Heritage Foundation, federal spending rose from "3.4% of GDP in 1930 to 6.9% in 1932 and reached 9.8% by 1940. That same year—10 years into the Great Depression—America's unemployment rate stood at 14.6%." In sum, massive increases in government spending did not result in noticeable economic improvements.

Even if infrastructure spending were to have positive effects, an early analysis of the Congressional Budget Office found that just 7% would be spent by next fall, with only 64% reaching the economy by 2011—likely after the country has entered into recovery.

4. *Japan's "lost decade."* Japan's "lost decade" of economic growth of the 1990s presents an excellent case study for the suggested package. Over a period of seven years, the government implemented eight different, large stimulus packages much like Obama has proposed.

The government must instead institute wide-ranging, permanent, pro-growth tax rate cuts, starting with making the [George W.] Bush tax cuts permanent and expanding them.

According to the *Wall Street Journal*, during the 1990s, the Japanese government, faced with many of the problems we are confronted with today, tried giving out loans to businesses, boosting infrastructure spending, buying bad assets off of banks and distributing tax rebates, among other Obama-esque policies.

These policies resulted in an increase in Japan's debt-to-GDP ratio from 68.6% in 1992 to 128.3% in 1999. In essence, government spending in Japan skyrocketed in ways very similar to Obama's proposals, yet the economy did not experience noticeable improvements until the current decade.

5. *An alternative proposal.* The government must instead institute wide-ranging, permanent, pro-growth tax rate cuts, starting with making the [George W.] Bush tax cuts permanent and expanding them. Beginning in 2010, the Bush rate reductions on income, capital gains (investments) and the estate tax will start to dissipate. With the dire need for capital

injections into the market, allowing the 15% capital gains rate to return to the 20% rate would discourage investment in the economy. Instead, the capital gains tax should at least be cut in half to 7.5%, if not temporarily expunged for all investments begun this year and kept for no less than two years, so as to incentivize greater investment.

Former House Speaker Newt Gingrich has proposed that the 25% income tax rate be reduced to 15%, thereby "establish[ing] a flat-rate tax of 15% for close to 90% of workers." Such targeted tax cuts would give the economy the boost it needs to create jobs and increase consumer demand and investment. We must then slice the corporate tax rate from 35%, the second highest in the world, to 25%, the average in Europe. This would expand incentives for businesses to create jobs in America and lessen the enticement to outsource.

If the Bush tax cuts expire, taxpayers will reduce spending in anticipation of the expirations, stunting the benefits of the rebates further. Alternatively, the knowledge that tax rates will be cut and individuals will be permitted to keep more of their income will give a sense of comfort to the beneficiaries.

By cutting marginal tax rates now, the short-term effect will be a rise in consumer confidence, resulting in a boost in consumer spending. Despite popular misconception that the Bush tax cuts did not work, the long-term relief that came in the form of broad-based tax rate reductions in 2003 resulted in the largest single-quarter GDP growth in 20 years, 7.2%, and the creation of 8 million new jobs through 2007.

The president has disappointingly labeled such contentions against his plan "old," "phony," "worn out" and "tired." Yet history has shown that the net benefit of such stimulus packages is minimal, and he who does not learn from history is doomed to repeat it.

A fiscal stimulus of tax rate cuts, not tax rebates or infrastructure spending, would stimulate an economic recovery by putting more money in people's pockets long term and increasing demand in the short term. That is the kind of economic policy that would do America the most good.

Health Care Reform Is a Vital Part of Economic Recovery

New America Foundation

The New America Foundation is a nonprofit, nonpartisan public policy institute that seeks to address the next generation of challenges facing the United States.

Our nation's health system is in crisis. Forty-six million Americans are uninsured and millions more are paying more than they can afford for health insurance that does not satisfy their health and financial needs. In the midst of economic uncertainty, U.S. businesses are losing ground to their foreign competitors and rising health care costs are placing increasing strain on federal, state, and local governments. Meanwhile, the American health system is fraught with errors and uncoordinated medical care.

Some say that now is not the right time to reform our health care system because of the worldwide economic downturn. No statement could be more wrong. Our social and economic futures depend upon creating a sustainable health care system. To postpone health care reform would be unwise. Our system cannot be transformed overnight. But to achieve success we must begin to invest in a quality, 21st-century health system today.

America can do better. Comprehensive health reform that ensures all Americans have quality, affordable health coverage, controls health care spending over time, and improves the quality of patient care is a moral and economic imperative. A sustainable system of coverage that includes every American will make our health system work better for us all. . . .

New America Foundation, *The Case for Health Reform: The Moral, Economic, & Quality Motives for Action.* Washington, DC: New America Foundation, 2009. Copyright © 2008 New America Foundation. Reproduced by permission.

America cannot afford our current health system any longer. Rising health care costs threaten the economic future of employers, workers, government, and American households.

The income and productivity our economy loses every year because of the poor health ... of the uninsured is as much as ... the public cost of covering all Americans.

More and more Americans find quality health care coverage simply unaffordable. The share of median family income spent on family health insurance jumped from 7.3 percent in 1987 to 16.8 percent in 2006. Worse yet, the full cost of family employer-sponsored health insurance will be more than $24,000 in 2016. This means half of American households would need to spend more than one-third of their income to buy health insurance for themselves and their families. These cost-to-income trajectories cannot be sustained.

- From 1999 to 2007, employee health insurance contributions rose by 102 percent.

- In 2006, one-fifth of the nation spent more than 10 percent of their income on out-of-pocket medical expenses.

- The average deductible will reach nearly $2,700 in 2016—almost doubling the amount Americans will have to spend before their insurance begins to pay for their medical care.

We must reform our nation's health care system—not despite our economic crisis, but precisely because of the impact it has on U.S. workers and businesses. The income and productivity our economy loses every year because of the poor health and shorter lifespan of the uninsured is as much as and perhaps greater than the public cost of covering all Americans.

- The U.S. economy lost more than $207 billion in 2007 because of the poor health and shorter lifespan of the uninsured. This is over $4,500 per uninsured resident— more than the cost of providing that person quality health coverage. This calculation does not take into account other spillover costs.

U.S. businesses and hard-working Americans are suffering. The employer health care burden makes it difficult for employers to compete in the 21st-century global economy. Rising health care costs threaten the profitability of U.S. businesses, the stability of American jobs, and workers' wages. In addition, globalization makes it impossible for firms to shift health care costs into the prices of their goods. As a result, employers are reducing or eliminating health benefits and workers are paying a larger share of the bill.

- Manufacturing firms in the United States pay more than twice as much in hourly health costs as their major trading partners—$2.38 per worker per hour versus $0.96.

- The percentage of employers offering health benefits has declined from 69 percent to 60 percent since 2000. Over the same period, the average worker contribution for family coverage increased by 102 percent, while average wages only increased by 3 percent.

- The United States spends upwards of 15 percent of GDP [gross domestic product, a measure of a country's total economic output] on health expenditures and more than $6,000 per capita. Our major trading partners like Japan, France, Germany, Canada, and the U.K. [United Kingdom] spend between 7.8 percent and 10.6 percent of GDP and $2,300 and $3,200 per capita on health care.

The consequences stemming from a lack of health insurance only worsen during slow economic times.

- A 1 percentage point rise in the unemployment rate would increase Medicaid and SCHIP [State Children's Health Insurance Program] enrollment by 1 million and cause the number of uninsured to grow by 1.1 million. That change would increase total Medicaid and SCHIP costs by $3.4 billion, which includes $1.4 billion in state spending.

- The health insurance subsidies included in the American Recovery and Reinvestment Act will lessen the potential increases in the uninsured; however, we will likely still see an increase in the uninsured as a result of the current economic downturn. We have much work left to do to solve the underlying, long-term problems of our health care system.

The insured have higher health care bills. Families across America pay a "hidden tax" to provide health care to the uninsured. When medical bills go unpaid, providers attempt to recoup the lost revenues by raising the rates for services delivered to the privately insured. As a result, insurers raise premiums. This vicious cycle inextricably links the uninsured to health care costs and by extension premium rates. . . .

- While estimates vary, the hidden tax is likely between 3–11 percent of health care premiums. In terms of premium costs, this adds between $360 and $1300 to the price of a family's health insurance coverage per year.

Workers are less productive. The uninsured are more likely to be sick unnecessarily for long periods of time. Poor health decreases workplace productivity.

- The loss in workplace productivity stemming from poor health reduces total productive work hours by as much as one-fifth. For an employee working 40 hours a week, this equates to as much as 4 days a month in lost work time.

- A case study of Dow Chemical Company shows that productivity losses from depression were greater than the total losses from the cost of medical care, missed work days, and decreases in on-the-job productivity as a result of all other chronic conditions.

Health care costs jeopardize the financial stability of our government. Rising health care costs place increasing strain on state and local budgets and threaten the sustainability of the Medicare and Medicaid programs. Health care is consuming a greater and greater share of the federal budget. Over time, health care spending could endanger other vital spending priorities or continue to increase our federal deficits.

- Former CBO [Congressional Budget Office] director and current OMB [Office of Management and Budget] director Peter Orszag has said consistently that rising health care costs are the largest threat to our nation's long-term fiscal future.

- By 2035, health care spending will account for more than 30 percent of U.S. GDP—double its current share of 15 percent.

- Medicaid accounted for 21.2 percent of state spending in 2007, an increase of more than 6 percent over 2006.

- Medicare reform is the key to fiscal sustainability. The key to Medicare reform is creating a more value-based, efficient delivery system. Delivery system reform is a necessary complement to coverage expansion. Therefore, health care reform is inextricably linked to a more fiscally sustainable Medicare program and a sound federal budget.

The cost of health reform is small relative to the potential gain. While genuine reform will require new spending in the short run, the economic and social cost of inaction are high and they will only rise over time.

- The funding necessary to finance comprehensive health reform is credibly estimated to be about 1 percent of GDP ($140 billion in 2007).

- Health care spending that does not add clinical value accounts for 5 percent of GDP. Reducing this unnecessary spending by one-fifth could pay for covering the uninsured.

- CMS [Centers for Medicare & Medicaid Services] projects that total health spending in 2016 will be $4 trillion. If we could cut spending that does not add clinical value by just 10 percent per year for 10 years, total health spending would be $900 billion lower. That is $900 billion that we could spend on the uninsured, education, infrastructure, energy independence, defense, and other national priorities.

Immigration Reform Is Essential for Long-Term Economic Growth

American Chronicle

American Chronicle *is an online news magazine.*

Immigration reform will be essential to supporting entitlements and long-term economic growth. That was the message that came out of a Capitol Hill forum today [May 20, 2009] convened by the nonpartisan Reform Institute. The institute is seeking to transform the immigration debate and advance reforms that enhance the vitality and resilience of the U.S. economy. The discussion featured former U.S. Commerce Secretary Carlos Gutierrez and prominent demographer Dr. Dowell Myers of the University of Southern California.

The Economic Value of Immigrants

"The United States has long benefited from having the most talented, hardest working labor force; fixing our broken immigration system so that the best and the brightest from around the globe will continue to bring their energy and entrepreneurial spirit to the U.S. will be critical to maintaining our competitive edge as well as our ability to be the land of opportunity and prosperity," stated Secretary Gutierrez. "I am pleased to work with the Reform Institute to promote comprehensive immigration reform that strengthens the economy for all Americans."

As the United States recovers from the current recession it will face an even more profound economic challenge in the aging of the baby boom generation. As the boomers retire in a few short years, the shift will be like a tsunami that could

American Chronicle, "Immigration Reform Can Bolster the Economy," May 20, 2009. Reproduced by permission.

overwhelm the federal budget and entitlement programs, the workforce, and the housing market. Sensible immigration policy that encourages an infusion of workers from abroad will help mitigate the effects of an aging society on the U.S. economy.

"The two greatest demographic forces that will shape America's future are the aging of the baby boomers and the settlement and advancement of immigrants; where they intersect must be a key focus for policy makers," according to Dr. Myers. "We cannot afford to continue to treat these phenomena as separate." Dr. Myers is author of the award-winning book *Immigrants and Boomers: Forging a New Social Contract for the Future of America,* as well as the Reform Institute white paper, *Old Promises and New Blood: How Immigration Reform Can Help America Prosper in the Face of Baby Boomer Retirement.*

The forum was a part of the Reform Institute's ongoing efforts to achieve fundamental reform that balances security and enforcement with acknowledging the contributions of immigrants to our economy and society. The institute promotes civil discourse and bipartisan collaboration toward meaningful reform.

"Comprehensive immigration reform must be a part of comprehensive efforts to strengthen the economy and entitlements," according to Reform Institute executive director Cecilia Martinez, who moderated the discussion. "The White House and Congress must recognize the importance of immigration to the U.S. economy and pursue reform in conjunction with efforts to spur the economy instead of using the economy as an excuse to delay action."

The United States Must Embark on a Sweeping Program of Structural Modernization

Michael Lind

Michael Lind is an author; a senior fellow at the New America Foundation, a public policy institute; and the policy director of New America's Economic Growth Program.

The inauguration of Barack Obama as president of the United States, along with the deepening of the Democratic majorities in both houses of Congress, marks more than a shift in the pendulum swings of partisan politics. In these pages I have suggested that it marks the dawn of a Fourth American Republic, in the way that the New Deal marked the beginning of Franklin Roosevelt's Third Republic of the United States and the Civil War and Reconstruction began [Abraham] Lincoln's Second Republic.

When Franklin Roosevelt was inaugurated, he had adopted the popular writer Stuart Chase's phrase "a New Deal," even though the contents of that New Deal were yet to be determined. In the absence of consensus on a similar term for the Age of Obama, we might draw on America's tradition of contractarian language—the New Deal, the Fair Deal, the Square Deal, the New Covenant, the Contract with America—and call this new period the era of the New Contract. That serves as well as any other name as a title for a synthesis of the three new strategies that the United States needs in the next generation: the Next American System, a new economic growth

Michael Lind, "The Next American System: We Need a New Contract with the American People, Starting with a Sweeping Program of Modernization that Echoes Lincoln and FDR," Salon.com, January 20, 2009. www.salon.com. This article first appeared in Salon.com, at http://www.salon.com. An online version remains in the Salon archives. Reprinted with permission.

agenda; the Citizen-Based Social Contract, the completion of America's incomplete system of social insurance; and a New American Internationalism, based on a strategy of concert among the great powers. I don't expect the New Contract to be adopted as proposed. My purpose is to start a debate, not offer a prophecy.

[The economic crisis requires] a return to old-fashioned American-style developmental capitalism.

In this [viewpoint] . . . I will explore the Next American System. The Next American System is the 21st-century equivalent of [19th-century statesman] Henry Clay's and Abraham Lincoln's American System, a program for modernizing the U.S. by promoting canals and railroads, steam-powered factories and national banking. It is also a version for our time of the program of the mid-20th-century New Deal era for promoting economic recovery, exports, rural electrification, and highway construction.

Eliminating the Trade Deficit

Beginning in the 1970s, conservatives and centrist liberals shared the delusion that government was the problem and the self-regulating market the solution; neoliberal Democrats simply wanted more after-tax redistribution to compensate the market economy's losers. The economic crisis, which is resulting in the partial nationalization of the banking sector and industries like automobile production, should forever discredit this kind of [Ronald] Reagan-to-[former Treasury secretary Robert] Rubin market utopianism. The alternative is not socialism or a mere revival of Keynesianism [ideas of John Maynard Keynes, a British economist]. It is a return to old-fashioned American-style developmental capitalism, which existed in both Lincoln Republican and Roosevelt Democrat forms. In developmental capitalism the government is viewed not as a neutral umpire between American producers and foreign producers, but as the coach of a mostly private team—America Inc. Success in the game will make future debt-financed bailouts less likely and less necessary.

Even a successful [economic] stimulus will merely return us to the world of chronic trade imbalances . . . unless it is accompanied by a rebalancing of the world economy.

Beyond the stimulus, the priority of U.S. economic policy in the Obama years must be to avert future bubbles like the tech bubble and the housing bubble by addressing one of the root causes. That is the interaction between the chronic trade deficits of the United States and the chronic trade surpluses of China, Japan, Germany and the oil-exporting countries. The surplus U.S. dollars that those trade surplus nations have accumulated, invested in U.S. Treasury bills and other financial assets, made possible low U.S. interest rates, which in turn lowered the cost of borrowing to reckless speculators in tech stocks, mortgages and gold. Even a successful stimulus will merely return us to the world of chronic trade imbalances and the resulting bubbles and busts unless it is accompanied by a rebalancing of the world economy, in which the United States makes and exports more manufactured goods and the trade surplus nations export less and consume more. As [economist] Paul Krugman among others has argued, a "plausible route to sustained recovery would be a drastic reduction in the U.S. trade deficit, which soared at the same time the housing bubble was inflating. By selling more to other countries and spending more of our own income on U.S.-produced goods, we could get to full employment without a boom in either consumption or investment spending."

While pressuring the surplus nations to end unfair mercantilism and increase consumption, the U.S. must shift capital and labor from low-value-added industries like restaurants and retail to high-value-added manufacturing, high-value services, and research and development. Export-oriented, import-competing industries like automobiles and aerospace tend to have much higher productivity growth and R&D [research and development] spending than other industries. Manufacturing-led growth for both the United States and global markets can melt away the debt legacy of today's economic emergency more rapidly.

The United States should lower or abolish its high corporate income tax. . . . This would stimulate foreign direct investment in U.S. production.

Tax Changes

In the new era of American developmental capitalism, the tax code will have two purposes—raising adequate revenue and promoting "onshoring" or the growth of high-value-added production inside U.S. borders, by domestic and foreign companies alike. To encourage onshoring, the United States should lower or abolish its high corporate income tax, one of the few sound ideas of the American right. This would stimulate foreign direct investment in U.S. production. It would also reduce the incentive for U.S. companies to engage in tax avoidance schemes.

If the corporate income tax remains, then, as the economist Ralph Gomory has suggested, it should be made variable and lowered for high-value-added production inside the United States. Alternately, the United States could replace the corporate income tax with a value-added tax (VAT). This would level the playing field for American companies. They are punished by de facto tariffs in the form of VATs in Europe and Asia, even as European and Asian exporters get government subsidies in the form of VAT rebates from their governments. In addition, a "Gomory VAT" could be reduced for high-value-added U.S. production, regardless of the nationality of the company or investors.

Adding a VAT to the mix of federal taxes would shift the United States toward the European mix of national consumption, payroll and income taxes. In the next half-century, even after runaway health care costs are controlled, the U.S. government share of GDP [gross domestic product, a measure of a country's economic output], while remaining relatively low by international standards, needs to expand by several percentage points to pay for universal health care, adequate retirement and a permanently higher level of infrastructure investment. Invisible taxes like payroll and consumption taxes are a better way to finance modern big government than highly visible taxes like income taxes and property taxes. Because they do not cause "sticker shock" to check writers around April 15 or when mortgage payments are due, they are harder for politicians to inveigh against on the campaign trail. Consumption and payroll taxes tend to be regressive in their effect on middle- and low-income people. But the exemption of necessities from consumption taxes, payroll tax rebates or (better yet) allowing biweekly credits against payroll tax withholding, an idea I have suggested elsewhere, can make these taxes more progressive.

[The United States should] build an intercontinental electric freight and passenger rail system . . . and a smart, green, national electric grid.

A New Energy and Transportation Policy

To promote high-tech domestic manufacturing as the engine that will drive U.S. economic growth, America's energy policy must reduce greenhouse gas emissions in an industry-friendly way. This can be done by means of a federal oil and gas trigger-price system that provides stable energy prices for industry even as it supports alternate energy development. If the price of gas falls below a floor, gas taxes will increase, so that long-term investments in alternative energy sources will not be wiped out. If the price of gas rises above a ceiling, then a new U.S. civilian strategic petroleum reserve will flood the market to lower them.

Transportation is responsible for two-thirds of U.S. petroleum consumption. The answer is not to throw money at crash programs for this or that single technology—ethanol, solar, wind. It is to build an intercontinental electric freight and passenger rail system to reduce reliance on trucks, cars and airplanes—and a smart, green, national electric grid, open to a variety of clean energy sources, that can power the electric trains and, perhaps, in time, a hybrid or purely electric automobile fleet.

"Internal improvements" in the form of federally financed canals and railroads were part of the Clay-Lincoln American System. Long-overdue infrastructure investment must be part of the Next American System—not only "shovel-ready projects" as part of the short-term stimulus, but a permanent commitment to green and high-tech energy, transportation and telecommunications grids. These are classic capital improvements that should be paid for by borrowing rather than upfront spending. President Obama supports a National Infrastructure Reinvestment Bank. Allowing such an infrastructure bank and similar federal economic development agencies to issue bonds, as state and local governments and agencies routinely do, would permit the federal government to channel private international capital and even money from foreign sovereign wealth funds into productivity-enhancing public investments, without selling or leasing U.S. infrastructure assets to foreign corporations or governments.

An Active Federal Labor Policy

Only a minority of Americans are likely to be employed directly in manufacturing. Even so, a new American developmental capitalism requires an active federal labor market policy that aims to shift labor out of low-productivity industries like retail and restaurants and into the goods-producing export sector and its supporting industries. If labor is to be diverted from wasteful low-productivity jobs into the traded-goods export sector, service sector wages need to be much higher. Congress should pass pro-union legislation, but at best, it would take decades to rebuild the labor movement in the private sector. We don't have the time. The federal government should intervene directly, gradually raising the minimum wage until it is an inflation-adjusted living wage of $10 or more an hour.

Wouldn't a high minimum-wage policy destroy some jobs in the service sector? Let's hope so. Minimizing the number of menial jobs—gradually, not all at once—is the whole point. There would, however, be no wave of outsourcing as a result of higher service sector wages, because most nontraded service sector jobs like nursing can be performed only in the United States. One beneficial side effect of this policy would be an incentive to automate backward, labor-intensive sectors like hospitals and home construction. Another would be increased demand for U.S.-made goods by well-paid American workers. Higher wages need not lead to inflation as long as productivity growth increases—in part as a result of the substitution of capital for more expensive labor

To further discourage employment in less-productive sectors, Congress should impose a federal servant tax on the employers of nannies, maids, gardeners, chauffeurs, restaurant and hotel workers and other menial servants in luxury industries. That labor could be more productively employed to the benefit of the nation in the export sector or non-luxury services like health care, elder care and education. We need more machinists and fewer maids. In a democratic republic, even affluent citizens should not be too good to take out the trash and mop the floor themselves. Middle-class and low-income Americans unable to afford necessary services like nursing could be given vouchers or tax credits, or those could be publicly provided.

Immigration Reforms

The American growth agenda requires an immigration policy in the national interest. A policy of enhancing productivity growth by gradually raising wages in the service sector cannot succeed if unpatriotic employers can sabotage it. This means eliminating the ability of employers to pit illegal aliens or indentured servants like H-1B's [a category of temporary U.S. visa] against American citizens and legal immigrants. Most of today's illegal immigrants should be quickly made citizens with full rights—but only after illegal immigration has been reduced to a trickle, by a national ID [identification] card system, severe employer sanctions and a combination of border fencing and enhanced border patrols. Meanwhile, indentured servitude in the United States should be outlawed by abolishing programs like the H-1B visa, which makes foreign workers dependent on their employers, and replacing it with a skills quota like those of the U.K. [United Kingdom] and Canada. Unlike H-1B's, qualified applicants would get green cards at once and compete on fair terms with American workers and legal permanent residents. Under no circumstances should the U.S. Chamber of Commerce be given its sinister "guest worker" program, which is really a colossal serf-worker program.

Most of these sensible immigration reforms were recommended in 1996 by President [Bill] Clinton's Commission on Immigration Reform, headed by [professor and former member of Congress] Barbara Jordan. President Obama and Congress should abandon the misguided [Senator Ted] Kennedy-

[Senator John] McCain comprehensive immigration reform approach, with its dangerous concessions to the cheap-labor lobby, and move quickly to enact the decade-old recommendations of the Jordan commission instead.

I'll conclude this discussion of a new growth agenda with the words of Barbara Jordan at the Democratic National Convention in 1992: "Why not change from a party with a reputation of tax and spend to one with a reputation of investment and growth? . . . A growth economy is a must. We can grow the economy and sustain an improved environment at the same time. When the economy is growing and we are taking care of our air and soil and water, we all prosper. And we can do all of that."

Policy Makers Must Adopt a New Regulatory Framework to Prevent Future Financial Abuses

Martin Neil Baily and Robert E. Litan

Martin Neil Baily and Robert E. Litan are senior fellows in economic studies for the Brookings Institution, a public policy think tank.

The financial crisis that began in 2007 has triggered a deep and troubling recession that has become a searing experience for Americans and everyone in the global economy. Trillions of dollars of wealth—in stocks, housing values, and in assets held by a wide range of financial institutions—have disappeared. Employment has been falling since December 2007, the official start-date of the recession, and the number of payroll jobs has fallen by 3.6 million through January 2009 and seems likely to fall much more before the economy turns. Unemployment increased to 7.6 percent in January and threatens to move over 10 percent. The unemployment rate will not start down again until GDP [gross domestic product, a measure of a country's economic output] grows faster than about 2.5 percent a year. Even with the record-setting fiscal stimulus that Congress is likely to approve shortly [the American Recovery and Reinvestment Act was approved by Congress on February 13, 2009, and signed into law by President Obama on February 17] and continuing purchases of mortgage and other securities by the Federal Reserve [the Fed, the nation's central bank] to enhance liquidity, the economy is unlikely to grow at that pace until later this year, or more likely, some time in 2010. By that point, the recession will have been the longest, and perhaps the deepest when measured from peak to trough, in the 63 years since the end of World War II.

Behind these statistics lie millions of human beings: those who have lost or will lose their jobs, their homes, their health insurance, and in many cases their dignity and hope. Millions more nervously worry about their own economic futures, and those of their children.

Origins of the Financial Crisis

All of this is shocking in its own right, but even more so because of its suddenness. Only a few short years ago (which now seems an eternity), policy makers and many in the economics profession were celebrating the "Great Moderation"— the roughly 25 years of reasonably steady growth without high or accelerating inflation that followed the Fed's successful anti-inflationary drive of the early 1980s. To be sure, there were scary bumps in the road, but each time a crisis threatened (the stock market crash of October 1987 and the Asian/ Russian financial crises of 1997–98) or a shallow recession intervened (1991–92 and 2000–01), the Fed was able to prevent the worst by loosening monetary policy, giving rise to what commonly became known as the "Greenspan put." The economy was also able to weather the savings and loan and banking crises of the 1980s and early 1990s, as policy makers eventually closed failed institutions (or merged them with healthier partners) and strengthened market discipline by imposing capital standards on depository institutions and enforcing a new system of "prompt corrective action" (PCA) that imposed progressively stiff sanctions on institutions that failed to meet these standards. Even after the Internet stock bubble burst in April 2000, and the financial scandals of the late 1990s and earlier this decade surfaced—Enron, WorldCom, Tyco and others—the economy and the equities market both rebounded.

But then a harsh reality intervened. In 2006, the now all-too-obvious bubble in housing prices began to burst, and the Great Moderation started to unravel. At first, the damage seemed to be limited to the securities backed by "subprime mortgages," but as the losses from these complex instruments cascaded throughout the global financial system, other weaknesses have surfaced. Like dominoes falling on a card table, other segments of the financial system—securities backed by other types of assets (commercial mortgages, auto loans and credit cards), corporate and municipal bonds, and equities— began to buckle. And so did many financial institutions that had invested in (and assembled and issued) these securities. Once household names in finance—Merrill Lynch, Washington Mutual, AIG, Bear Stearns, Lehman Brothers, Wachovia, Fannie Mae and Freddie Mac—disappeared, were propped up by the government, or forced to merge with other institutions, at a stunning rate.

This [economic] crisis has ... powerfully demonstrated the fragility of finance.

A Loss of Trust

We knew all along how interconnected our modern financial system was and remains—among and between the institutions and markets in this country, and those of other countries. But this crisis has also powerfully demonstrated the fragility of finance: how the trust on which it depends can evaporate in short order, especially for institutions that are highly leveraged and thus highly susceptible to insolvency when asset losses start to mount. At the height of the financial boom, investors seeking high returns seemed willing almost to ignore the risks of loss or default in the assets they were buying—the risk premium fell well below its normal historical level. The implosion of asset values in equities and real estate markets since then reflects a loss of trust, as investors flee to "safe assets"—Treasury bonds and their equivalents, insured depository institution accounts barely paying any interest—rather than hold their wealth in financial instruments issued by private companies or in residential or commercial real estate properties. Clearly, the pendulum has swung back and the risk premium is now very high. The extraordinary Bernard Madoff [Ponzi scheme] scandal that surfaced as 2008 came to a close seemed an apt symbol of the times: even wealthy, and some sophisticated investors and money managers can be duped, along with the regulators who were supposed to be watching. "Who can we trust?" is a question that many even not-so-wealthy investors must now be asking.

It is not only individuals who have lost faith in finance. Banks around the world lost trust in other banks and so the market in interbank lending nearly collapsed this past fall [2008], until it was rescued through capital injections in banks under the Troubled Asset [Relief] Program (TARP) and continued lending and asset purchases by the Federal Reserve.

President Obama's Challenge

All eyes are now turned on Washington and to the new administration of President [Barack] Obama. The immediate economic challenge is to revive the banks so that normal lending can resume and to stem the free fall of the real economy of jobs and production. But there is also the longer-term challenge of reforming the supervision and regulation of the financial sector in order to reduce the chances of another financial crisis in the future. This crisis has been a sobering experience. No one wants to return to business as usual after the immediate crisis is over.

The Obama administration has announced that fixing the nation's financial system is one of its highest initial priorities and will shortly release a plan to do that. The administration's plan will follow a steady stream of prior work and reports:

- The chairmen of the two congressional committees through which new reform legislation must pass—the Senate Banking Committee and the House Financial Services Committee—have been working on financial reform since well before the election.

- The Bush Treasury Department anticipated the need for comprehensive financial reform legislation when it issued a *Blueprint for a Stronger Regulatory Structure* in March, 2008.

- More recently, both the Group of Thirty (an influential group of financial experts cochaired by [former Federal Reserve chairman] Paul Volcker) and the Congressional Oversight Panel (created in October 2008 to oversee the Troubled Asset [Relief] Program, or "TARP") have issued sweeping reports outlining ways to fix the financial system.

As the new administration and the Congress go about their work this year, the whole world will be watching. In mid-November [2008], the United States joined with other country members of the G-20 [a group of the world's wealthiest nations] to announce a global effort to revise the architecture for our increasingly global financial system. U.S. policy makers seemed intent on having at least the broad outlines of a reform package to present at the follow-up to that meeting, scheduled for April 2, 2009 in London.

In this [viewpoint], we attempt to provide our own version of a road map for reform. We will not pretend to cover every issue that legislators and regulators are likely to address, although we believe we spotted most of the main ones. . . .

A Road Map for Reform

We are in this mess today for multiple reasons. Private and public actors held the mistaken belief that residential real estate prices would continue rising, especially at a faster pace than the growth in the economy. Financial institutions, their executives and shareholders, exploited crevices in the financial regulatory system without regard to the cumulative damage they would eventually cause to the financial system. Regulators failed to police this activity, while both lawmakers and regulators failed to adapt financial rules to prevent the untoward side effects of rapid and increasingly complex financial innovations in mortgage markets specifically and financial markets more generally.

The central challenge confronting policy makers now is to establish a new regulatory framework that will do a far better job preventing financial abuses and their consequences without chilling innovation and prudent risk-taking that are essential for growth in any economy. To accomplish that end will require a major restructuring and strengthening of the two pillars upon which an efficient and safe financial system must rest: *market discipline* and *sound regulation*. It would be a mistake, in our view, to conclude that because both these pillars failed to prevent the current crisis that either one should be jettisoned. Neither pillar alone can do the job. There is no alternative, we need both pillars, but both need to work much better in the future.

In brief, here, we believe, is how:

1. *Multiple measures should be adopted to improve transparency and increase the incentive for prudent behavior throughout the mortgage process*: at loan origination (especially for mortgage borrowers), by mortgage originators and securitizers, and by credit rating agencies. Mortgage securitizers should be required to retain some of the risk of the mortgages they package and distribute as securities. They would then have an incentive to ensure that mortgage holders can actually make their monthly payments. Federal standards should apply to all mortgage originations by all financial institutions, whether regulated at the federal or state level. This

would prevent mortgage brokers from creating misleading products that borrowers do not understand and cannot service. And credit rating agencies should be held to new methods of reporting that should make them more accountable to the marketplace.

2. *A special set of prudential rules should govern the regulation of systemically important financial institutions (SIFIs)*, or those whose failure could have systemic consequences, and thus trigger federal rescues. These rules should take account of the differences in the types of institutions and should include higher capital and liquidity requirements, and a system of early, prompt resolution in lieu of traditional bankruptcy (which should significantly reduce, but entirely eliminate, the need for future federally financed rescues). In addition, all financial regulators, but especially the regulator charged with oversight of SIFIs, should be required to provide an annual report to Congress on the risks to the financial system posed by the institutions subject to their purview. We do not support reforms that would require federal agencies to screen financial innovations in advance; a far better approach, the one we generally take with other new products in our economy, is to monitor closely the impact of innovations after they are introduced into the marketplace, and if harms are occurring, regulate them in a cost-effective manner at that point.

3. *To harness stable, market discipline, the prudential regulator (discussed shortly) should require all SIFIs to fund some portion of their assets with long-term, subordinated debt.* Such debt might also be convertible to equity in the event the institution's capital-to-asset ratio falls below a certain level. Capital standards should be made counter-cyclical by requiring a higher capital cushion in

"good times" and allowing lower capital ratios in bad times. After all, if a bank takes losses on its asset portfolio and its capital declines as a result, this means the capital cushion is doing exactly what it is designed for.

4. *Regulators should encourage the formation of clearinghouses for derivatives contracts, starting with credit default swaps.* At the same time, Congress should authorize an overseer of derivatives markets to impose minimum capital and liquidity standards for such clearinghouses, while also setting minimum capital and collateral requirements for SIFIs that are counterparties to nonstandardized derivatives contracts that are not likely to be handled by clearinghouses.

5. *Financial reforms should be written broadly enough, and with enough discretion for regulators, so that policy makers can better anticipate future financial crises, however they might arise.* In this connection, bank regulators in particular can encourage, through their annual "CAMEL ratings," banks to use compensation systems that reward long-term performance rather than potentially misleading and risky short-run results. Regulators also should insist that financial institutions verify that their compensation practices are consistent with their internal risk management systems.

6. *The financial regulatory agencies should be reorganized*, so that they have jurisdiction by function or objective (solvency and consumer protection) rather than by type of charter of the regulated financial institution. This should improve financial regulation and eliminate jurisdictional overlaps. If a single solvency or prudential regulator is created for all financial institutions, it should set and enforce the special regulatory regime for SIFIs. The identification of SIFIs could be handled by the Federal Reserve, the solvency regulator, or both

jointly. However, financial regulation can be made significantly more effective if the other measures recommended here are implemented, even if the current financial regulatory structure is not reorganized.

7. *In the short to intermediate run, the housing GSEs [government sponsored enterprises]—Fannie Mae, Freddie Mac, and the Federal Home Loan Bank System—should be regulated as public utility "SIFIs" (after recapitalization with public funds) or directly operated as government agencies.* Any such plan should have an automatic sunset, perhaps after 5 or 10 years, with an orderly liquidation procedure implemented thereafter unless Congress specifically provides for some other outcome. Further, policy should promote affordable home ownership hereafter in a much more transparent fashion, through on-budget matching subsidies to assist homeowners in making down payments.

8. *U.S. financial policy makers must support international cooperation on financial regulation.* Most large financial institutions operate globally and there must be a mechanism for exchange of information and ideas among global regulators. In addition, there should be efforts to keep the playing field level for global competitors and to limit the ability of regulatory havens, such as the Cayman Islands, to undermine U.S. and global regulation. Given that the US originated this global crisis, however, we must get our own house in order. U.S. policy makers should not wait for international agreement before taking necessary steps to improve our own system.

Organizations to Contact

The editors have compiled the following list of organizations concerned with the issues debated in this book. The descriptions are derived from materials provided by the organizations. All have publications or information available for interested readers. The list was compiled on the date of publication of the present volume; the information provided here may change. Be aware that many organizations take several weeks or longer to respond to inquiries, so allow as much time as possible.

**American Enterprise Institute for
Public Policy Research (AEI)**
1150 Seventeenth Street NW, Washington, DC   20036
(202) 862-5800 • fax: (202) 862-7177
Web site: www.aei.org

The American Enterprise Institute for Public Policy Research (AEI) is a conservative think tank, founded in 1943 to defend the principles and improve the institutions of American freedom and democratic capitalism. AEI promotes limited government, private enterprise, individual liberty and responsibility, vigilant and effective defense and foreign policies, political accountability, and open debate. Economic policy is one of AEI's research areas and its Web site is a source of many books and publications relating to the U.S. economy. Recent articles include "Recession Blues" and "What Is Fiscally—and Politically—Sustainable?"

Brookings Institution
1775 Massachusetts Avenue NW, Washington, DC   20036
(202) 797-6000
Web site: www.brookings.edu

The Brookings Institution is a nonprofit public policy organization with a mission to conduct high-quality, independent research and to provide innovative, practical recommendations that advance three broad goals: (1) strengthening American democracy; (2) fostering the economic and social welfare, security, and opportunity of all Americans; and (3) securing a more open, safe, prosperous, and cooperative international system. The group's Web site contains a section on the economy, where numerous publications on the current recession can be found. Two recent examples include "The U.S. Financial and Economic Crisis: Where Does It Stand and Where Do We Go From Here?" and "Financial Globalization and Economic Policies."

Cato Institute
1000 Massachusetts Avenue NW
Washington, DC   20001-5403
(202) 842 0200 • fax: (202) 842 3490
Web site: www.cato.org

The Cato Institute is a nonprofit public policy research foundation known for its libertarian viewpoints. The foundation's mission is to increase the understanding of public policies based on the principles of limited government, free markets, individual liberty, and peace. The group's Web site provides an extensive list of publications dealing with various public policy issues, including economic matters. Cato also publishes papers in the *Cato Journal* three times per year, the quarterly magazine *Regulation*, and a bimonthly newsletter, *Cato Policy Report*. Recent publications include "The Limits of Monetary Policy" and "Monetary Policy and Financial Regulation."

Center for Global Development (CGD)
1800 Massachusetts Avenue NW, Third Floor
Washington, DC   20036
(202) 416-4000 • fax: (202) 416-4050
Web site: www.cgdev.org

The Center for Global Development (CGD) is an independent, nonprofit policy research organization dedicated to reducing global poverty and inequality and to making globalization work for the poor. The center conducts research and actively engages policy makers and the public to influence the policies of the United States, other wealthy countries, and financial institutions such as the World Bank, the International Monetary Fund (IMF), and the World Trade Organization (WTO) to improve the economic and social development prospects in poor countries. CGD's Web site contains a list of publications that includes articles such as "How the Economic Crisis Is Hurting Africa—And What to Do About It" and "Blunt Instruments: On Establishing the Causes of Economic Growth."

Center for the Study of Innovation and Productivity (CSIP)
Federal Reserve Bank of San Francisco, 101 Market Street
Mail Stop 1130, San Francisco, CA   94105
(415) 974-3198
e-mail: csip.info@sf.frb.org
Web site: www.frbsf.org

The Center for the Study of Innovation and Productivity (CSIP), organized under the Federal Reserve Bank of San Francisco's Economic Research Department, seeks to promote a better understanding of innovation and productivity and their links to the performance of national and regional economies in the United States. CSIP's core activity is research, but it also serves as a public resource, providing access to research, analysis, and selected data through the CSIP Web site.

Economic Policy Institute (EPI)
1333 H Street NW, Suite 300, East Tower
Washington, DC   20005-4707
(202) 775-8810 • fax: (202) 775-0819
e-mail: researchdept@epi.org
Web site: www.epi.org

The Economic Policy Institute (EPI) is a nonprofit Washington-based think tank created in 1986 to broaden the discussion about economic policy to include the interests of low- and middle-income workers. The group conducts research on the status of American workers and publishes a report called *State of Working America* every two years. The EPI Web site provides a list of publications, many of which concern U.S. economic matters. Examples of publications include "The Worst Downturn Since the Great Depression" and "Payback Time."

Federal Reserve System
Twentieth Street and Constitution Avenue NW
Washington, DC   20551
Web site: www.federalreserve.gov

The Federal Reserve System, also known as the Fed, was created by Congress in 1913 to be the nation's central bank. It is made up of a seven-member board of governors, a twelve-member Federal Open Market Committee, twelve regional member banks located throughout the United States, and staff economists. The Federal Reserve's function is to control inflation without triggering a recession. In addition, the Fed supervises the nation's banking system to protect consumers; maintains the stability of the financial markets to prevent potential crises; and acts as the central bank for other banks, the U.S. government, and foreign banks. The Fed's Web site is a source of economic research and data, and also provides consumer financial information.

Heritage Foundation
214 Massachusetts Avenue NE, Washington, DC   20002-4999
(202) 546-4400 • fax: (202) 546-8328
Web site: www.heritage.org

The Heritage Foundation is a conservative public policy research institute founded in 1973. Its mission is to formulate and promote conservative public policies based on the principles of free enterprise, limited government, individual freedom, traditional American values, and a strong national defense. The economy is one of the institute's issue areas, and its Web site is a source of economic publications, including "Republicans' Financial Regulatory Reform Plan a Good Start" and "Government Intervention: A Threat to Economic Recovery."

National Bureau of Economic Research (NBER)
1050 Massachusetts Avenue, Cambridge, Massachusetts 02138
(617) 868-3900
e-mail: info@nber.org
Web site: www.nber.org

Founded in 1920, the National Bureau of Economic Research (NBER) is a private, nonprofit, nonpartisan research organization that undertakes unbiased economic research among public policy makers, business professionals, and the academic community. A search of the NBER Web site produces numerous working papers and other information on various economic issues, including the 2009 recession. Examples of recent publications include "The Credit Rating Crisis" and "Inflation and the Stock Market: Understanding the 'Fed Model.'"

U.S. Department of the Treasury
1500 Pennsylvania Avenue NW, Washington, DC 20220
(202) 622-2000 • fax: (202) 622-6415
Web site: www.ustreas.gov

The Department of the Treasury is the executive agency responsible for promoting economic prosperity and ensuring the financial security of the United States. The Treasury is responsible for a wide range of activities, such as advising the president on economic and financial issues, encouraging sustainable economic growth, and fostering improved governance in financial institutions. The Treasury Department's Web site is a source of news and other information about the U.S. economy, including various government initiatives such as the Emergency Economic Stabilization Act, the Troubled Asset Relief Program (TARP), and other actions being taken to combat economic recession in the United States.

Bibliography

Books

Alan Beattie   *False Economy: A Surprising Economic History of the World*. New York: Riverhead Books, 2009.

Charles Brownell   *Subprime Meltdown: From U.S. Liquidity Crisis to Global Recession*. Scotts Valley, CA: CreateSpace, 2008.

Todd G. Buchholz and Martin Feldstein   *New Ideas from Dead Economists: An Introduction to Modern Economic Thought*. New York: Plume, 2007.

Gregory Clark   *A Farewell to Alms: A Brief Economic History of the World*. Princeton, NJ: Princeton University Press, 2007.

Niall Ferguson   *The Ascent of Money: A Financial History of the World*. New York: Penguin Press, 2008.

Sean Masaki Flynn   *Economics for Dummies*. Indianapolis, IN: For Dummies, 2008.

Benjamin M. Friedman   *The Moral Consequences of Economic Growth*. New York: Knopf, 2006.

Paul Krugman   *The Return of Depression Economics and the Crisis of 2008*. New York: W.W. Norton, 2009.

Robert Kuttner   *Obama's Challenge: America's Economic Crisis and the Power of a Transformative Presidency*. White River Junction, VT: Chelsea Green Publishing, 2008.

Charles R. Morris   *The Trillion Dollar Meltdown: Easy Money, High Rollers, and the Great Credit Crash*. New York: PublicAffairs, 2008.

Kevin Phillips   *Bad Money: Reckless Finance, Failed Politics, and the Global Crisis of American Capitalism*. New York: Viking, 2008.

Alessandro Roncaglia   *The Wealth of Ideas: A History of Economic Thought*. New York: Cambridge University Press, 2006.

Amity Shlaes   *The Forgotten Man: A New History of the Great Depression*. New York: Harper Perennial, 2008.

Thomas Sowell   *Basic Economics: A Common Sense Guide to the Economy*. New York: Basic Books, 2007.

Thomas E. Woods Jr.   *Meltdown: A Free-Market Look at Why the Stock Market Collapsed, the Economy Tanked, and Government Bailouts Will Make Things Worse*. Washington, DC: Regnery Publishing, 2009.

Periodicals

Frank Ahrens — "The Ticker: Actual U.S. Unemployment: 15.8%," *Washington Post*, May 8, 2009.

Rafael Alvarez — "Great Depression Icon Meets the Great Recession," *Christian Science Monitor*, March 24, 2009.

Jim Cooper — "Where Is the Economy Headed in 2009?" *Business Week*, December 17, 2008.

Richard Florida — "How the Crash Will Reshape America," *Atlantic*, March 2009.

Sy Harding — "Is the Recession Really Over?" StreetSmartReport.com, June 5, 2009. www.streetsmartreport.com.

Michael Hirsh — "Back from the Brink: Geithner May Have It Right After All," *Newsweek*, March 24, 2009.

Robert D. Hof — "Google: The Recession Takes Its Toll," *Business Week*, April 17, 2009.

Phil Izzo — "Obama, Geithner Get Low Grades from Economists," *Wall Street Journal*, March 11, 2009.

Alan B. Krueger — "A Future Consumption Tax to Fix Today's Economy," *New York Times*, January 12, 2009.

Paul Krugman — "Behind the Curve," *New York Times*, March 8, 2009.

David Leonhardt "After the Great Recession," *New York Times*, April 28, 2009.

Kimberly Palmer "Thriving During the Great Recession: How to Save More, Spend Less, and Still Enjoy Life's Luxuries," *U.S. News & World Report*, February 6, 2009.

The Progressive "The Great Recession," January 2009.

Ray Robison "How's Obama's Foreclosure Policy Working Out?" *American Thinker*, May 13, 2009.

Danny Schechter "The Age of Financial Reform or Plunder Without End?" *Global Research*, May 28, 2009.

Michael Scherer "Will Deficits Force Obama to Sacrifice His Agenda?" *TIME*, March 23, 2009.

Louis Uchitelle and Edmund L. Andrews "Economic Decline in Quarter Exceeds Forecast," *New York Times*, April 29, 2009.

Robert Wenzel "The Big Collapse Could Be Very Near," *Economic Policy Journal*, May 31, 2009.

Brian S. Wesbury and Robert Stein "The Recession Is Over," *Forbes*, May 5, 2009.

Peter Zeihan "The Geography of Recession," STRATFOR.com, June 6, 2009. www.stratfor.com.

Index

T

TALF. *See* Term Asset-Backed Securities Loan Facility

TARP. *See* Troubled Asset Relief Program

Taxes
    economic growth and, 142–146
    Gingrich's proposed tax policies, 88–89
    health care, 150
    income, 17
    lower taxes and increased spending, 107
    maximum tax rate, 122
    Obama's proposed tax policies, 83–88
    tax credits, 132
    tax cuts, 17, 23, 50, 56, 59, 65, 86, 95
    value-added tax, 158–159

Tent cities, 35–38

Term Asset-Backed Securities Loan Facility (TALF), 17, 70, 99

Toxic assets
    government absorption, 62–63, 69, 71, 75, 95, 99, 139
    stress tests, 33–34
    used as collateral, 99
    See also Derivatives

Trade, world, 43, 68

Trade deficit, 156–158

Transportation policy, 159–160

Treasury, U.S., 95

Treasury bonds, 90–91, 103, 111, 115, 124, 143, 157

Troubled Asset Relief Program (TARP), 17, 61, 69, 127, 167, 168

2010 Census, 45

Tyco, 165

U

Unemployment
    decreased rate, 17
    Great Depression, 26, 143–144
    increased rate, 16, 21, 43–44, 50–51, 52–53, 70, 72, 73, 74, 77, 82, 88, 94–95, 130, 131, 164
    insurance, 22
    layoff rate, 45–47
    newly unemployed, 27

United Kingdom, 40, 93, 149, 162

U.S. Chamber of Commerce, 162

U.S. Congress. *See* Congress

U.S. Debt. *See* Debt, U.S.

U.S. Federal Reserve. *See* Federal Reserve

U.S. Interagency Council on Homelessness, 37

U.S. Treasury, 95

V

Value-added tax (VAT), 158–159

Volcker, Paul, 134, 168

W

Wachovia, 166

Wages, 25–26

Wagoner, Rick, 95

Wall Street
    bonuses, 19
    earnings and wealth, 135, 164
    investors role in recession, 18
    overborrowing, 25
    political system and, 135–137
    PPIP and, 98
    recovery, 82
    regulation, 67